The Modern Soccer Coach 2014

A Four Dimensional Approach

Gary Curneen

BENNION
KEARNY

Published by Bennion Kearny Limited
6 Woodside
Churnet View Road
Oakamoor
Staffordshire
ST10 3AE

www.BennionKearny.com

Cover image: ©Shutterstock/Monkik
Inside images (as marked): ©Academy Soccer Coach

To Mum and Dad – You have allowed me to dream and encouraged me to follow them. You have given me everything you could, and more than I could ever have asked for.

To Angie – The best sister who is always just a phone call away.

To my wife Erin - Without your encouragement and love this book could not have been written.

Foreword

I have been involved in the game for over forty years as a player, coach, analyst, commentator and, most importantly, as a fan. The changes I have witnessed in football have been phenomenal on every level. However, as complex as the game is today, you cannot simply rely on one area of the game if you want to be successful at the highest level. Football coaching must take every aspect of the game into consideration. My experiences as a player in the 1982 and 1986 World Cups taught me the value of preparation. We did not have the big names of France, Spain, or Brazil, but we knew our strengths and embraced them. Belief and organization are paramount to winning any football match at World Cup level especially against the top teams in the world.

The game today is pure entertainment. Watching a Champions League game and seeing how players retain possession of the ball for long periods, then utilize their speed and firepower in attack, is so pleasing on the eye. It is easy to put the success down to skill alone but it takes more than that. Being technically superior to your opponents does not simply award you the right to win every time you step on the field. Spain were a technically better team than Northern Ireland in 1982 but it was in the psychological department where they had problems. They found it difficult to cope with the pressure of being strong favorites to win the World Cup. Also it was the first time they came up against a team so stubborn and well organized as we were. This frustration affected them greatly and we took advantage of that.

Do not let the skills and abilities of the Barcelona team today mislead you and classify them as a team who rely solely on technique. Under Pep Guardiola, they took football to another dimension in every department of the game. Of course, Messi was, and still is, at the forefront of this revolutionary style of play, but the team is only as strong as its weakest link. They play from the back, keep possession better than anyone else, and create one goalscoring opportunity after another. However, it is only possible because of the quality and mentality of Xavi, Busquets, Iniesta, Alves, Piqué, etc. The *tiki-taka* style celebrates hard work over anything else and you can tell this by how quickly they win the ball back; they almost starve the opposition of the ball. Most games I watched saw them have 70 per cent plus possession and their belief in their style gave them great confidence. They kept winning. Hard work, organization, belief, and confidence in each other allows Messi to flourish every week at the Nou Camp.

Training programs in La Liga have changed drastically since I was a player and are the main reason for the advancements in the speed, power, and skill that you see today. In my first preseason, with Real Mallorca, we did a running session on a golf course at 6.30am, followed by a weights session at 10.30am and then a third session at 7pm at the stadium incorporating ball work. I'm not sure many teams train like that today! Everything at the top clubs in modern football is geared towards maximizing the potential of the players in every aspect so we have seen the bar has been lifted on the coaching side too.

When Gary approached me about this book, I was very intrigued. I have known Gary and his father Sean for over twenty years, since the days of my Soccer School in Omagh, Northern Ireland, and have followed his path as a coach with keen interest. I meet a lot of people from all over the world who watch Spanish football and ask questions regarding transfer targets and who will be the next big player to burst onto the scene. When I talk to Gary however, the conversation always takes a slightly different path. He is keen to discuss European coaches and what makes them tick, wanting to know how the man-management is different, their approach to training, how they deal with the pressure from the press, and where I see the new developments in the game. His passion for the game is second to none and you can see he is always looking to add to his knowledge of the game, which successful coaches have to do.

Of course, realizing the game is different nowadays is one thing, but embracing it is quite another. A lot of my old teammates talk about the good old days when we played and, of course, I look back with fond memories. However, being successful today is about embracing all the new facets of the game. It is such an exciting time for football all over the world. National teams are improving, European competitions are becoming more competitive, and we are blessed with exciting new talents almost every season. Most importantly, however, is how coaches are dealing with this change. We have seen a new brand of coach at the top of European clubs. These coaches may be leading the way, but we need a new group of trailblazers. I urge any young coach who is ambitious in succeeding in this game to follow their lead. By investigating new methods, studying the best coaches, and experimenting with new sessions and exercises that can help develop players and teams alike. Gary's new book is a terrific guide on how to think and act if you want to be successful in the modern game. I highly recommend it and hope you enjoy both reading it and putting the ideas into practice with your team.

Gerry Armstrong

About the Author

 Gary is the current Head Women's Soccer Coach at California State University at Bakersfield. Prior to this, he was the Head Coach at Wingate University and Assistant Coach at University of Cincinnati. Gary holds a UEFA 'A' License from the Irish FA and 'Premier Diploma' from the NSCAA. Originally from Omagh, Northern Ireland, he gained a Master's in Business Administration from Wingate University. He is the author of *The Modern Soccer Coach 2014: A Four Dimensional Approach* and *The Modern Soccer Coach: Position-Specific Training*, as well as the children's book *Soccer Roy - First Touch*.

Acknowledgements

Thanks to the many coaches who have helped me complete this book, either through their direct assistance or indirect personal support; to Pat Sharkey, Marty Woodhead, Peter Bradley, and Dave Bell for teaching me what enthusiasm does for players; to Gary Hamill for setting an example of committing yourself fully to becoming a professional; to Neil Stafford and Nate Lie for their insights, and demanding more in every aspect of the game; and to Marty Gormley for his genius concepts on training sessions and practice plans. All of these coaches have inspired me to enjoy my work and always push for more.

I wish to acknowledge and thank Academy Soccer Coach for their work along with Bobby Puppione and Paul Kee for their contributions. I also have to thank Niall Donnelly and Ursula Donnelly who have dedicated much time and energy to help with website and design ideas.

Of course, this book would never have happened without the tireless work of the team at Bennion Kearny and my publisher James Lumsden-Cook, who I must thank for his patience, trust and invaluable help.

And finally, thanks to my family and friends in Wingate, Charlotte, Cincinnati, and, of course, Omagh, Northern Ireland. Like everything in life, you cannot go it alone and I am blessed to have a special group of people who make time and distance seem irrelevant.

Academy Soccer Coach

Academy Soccer Coach is a company that provides digital solutions for coaches at every level of the game. Our coaching software enables coaches, clubs and professional organizations to plan and prepare their sessions remotely from anywhere in the world.

Academy Soccer Coach works with following the professional clubs and organizations:

Fulham FC, West Ham United FC, Stoke FC, Newcastle United FC, Crystal Palace FC, Portland Timbers Sporting Kansas City, National Soccer Coaches Association of America, US Soccer (Women's), The Irish Football Association, The Professional Footballers Association, and many more.

For more information on Academy Soccer Coach and the services we provide please visit www.academysoccercoach.com

On a personal note we would like to wish Gary every success with his book and his continued growth and development as a coach.

The ASC Team

Illustrations (download)

If you are reading an electronic version of this book, you may find some of the illustrations difficult to explore fully on your Kindle or Nook or iPhone. Likewise, if you are reading the print version of the book and would like to get your hands on the illustrations anyway – we can help.

All the illustrations in this book are available as a freely downloadable PDF.

Download the file from the publisher's web page at:

www.bennionkearny.com/gc101.pdf

[Please note this web page address is case sensitive]

Table of Contents

1

Define Yourself

We've all felt it. That sinking feeling when the final whistle blows never truly goes away for a coach. After high hopes and real optimism, your team has just been comfortably beaten. It is that tough, introspective moment when you ask yourself "What could I have done differently?"

If you've stood on the sidelines you will know exactly what I mean. You have played against a team that you should have beaten and, for some reason, it did not come together. The performance was flat and your team got what they deserved. Family and friends don't know what to say and, in all honesty, you would rather they were not there to witness it.

As a coach, it is a lonely life sometimes and when the dust settles, you are normally left with three options: You can go into:

- Blame mode: the field, the ref, an incident, or a fixture congestion was the reason.

- Deflection mode: it wasn't our day, they had all the luck, or cling to perspective and say this will be good for us in the long-run.

- Or you can approach matters in a unique way and really look at your preparation, your training methods, your interaction with your players, and the way your team managed the game.

Coaches today must choose the third option if they want to be successful. The only thing guaranteed in soccer is that you will experience defeat and the longer you stay in the game, the better you have to become at dealing with it. A modern coach will solve his or her problems a lot quicker, and when the next game comes along, he/she will make sure that sinking feeling does not come back.

Soccer is the universal game with millions of coaches in different countries, working with players of different ages and different levels. The philosophies differ from coach to coach, but they all share two things in common. Firstly, a passion for the game that is unconditional, regardless of the result or the performance, or how bad it ever gets, we always come back for more. Secondly, and perhaps more objectively – coaches are all aiming for the 'promised land' - to have the hardest working team that can score at will with fast, free flowing soccer, and defend with equal effect using aggression and tenacity. In turn, they are looking to coach a team that exudes style and fluidity. We want people to watch our teams and go "wow!" We want people to be just as excited about the way we play than we as coaches are.

Coaches are very much aware that their team is a reflection of themselves. When our teams walk over the white line on a sunny Saturday or a cold, rainy, Wednesday, it is more than a game for the coach in charge. Everything your players do has your stamp on it like it is a personal work of art that you have produced. Coaches are artists and your team is your canvas. The way the players conduct themselves, how they interact, the style of play, and the result, are all ways that we measure the work of a coach.

Even in a world obsessed with results, the biggest disappointment for coaches will always be a poor performance. Sure, winning ugly in a cup semi-final will invariably be a sweet victory, but the majority of games we are all looking at the performance first and foremost. The reason for that is simple: *a result usually follows a good performance*. I am a big believer of this and always will be. As a coach myself, I have worked in college soccer for over ten years. I have coached on both female and male sides, and Division I and Division II. Like millions of other coaches, I have had good days at the office and an awful lot of bad ones. Throughout my journey as a coach, I have never reached the 'Promised Land'. I have never walked off a field thinking that my team have finally "got it" and mastered the game. Every week, however, when game day comes along, I wonder if this is it. Could this be the moment that my team produces the ultimate performance? When spectators compare us with the greatest teams ever to play the game. It has not arrived yet, and may never, but that never discourages me from thinking it is right around the corner. Some people believe coaching is all about glory and developing players, but in reality, it can be a series of disappointments and anticlimaxes. Just when the game shows us a glimpse of hope, we are dealt another setback. That is what makes it special though and keeps us coming back for more. Whoever said to "Focus on the journey and not the destination" must have been a great soccer coach.

My First Coaching Philosophy

I first began coaching in 2003, around the same time José Mourinho introduced himself to the football world with Porto and then Chelsea. Before he even announced himself as the "Special One", I was fascinated by him. The way he conducted himself on the sidelines and press conferences exuded self-confidence and there was no way his teams were going to lose. For me, he was a new style of coach and I wanted to be like him!

Mourinho helped shape my early coaching philosophy but I truly believe that during these years, something was missing from my work. In my discovery stage, everything about tactics and coaching was new and I began to study the game the right way. As a graduate assistant coach living on campus, my social life very much took a back seat for a couple of years and I grabbed the opportunity to fully commit myself to my new profession. I took my "UEFA A License" in Belfast and the education continued. I found myself on a course sitting alongside international and Premiership managers in a unique learning environment. I studied teams training and took regular visits to Premiership training grounds. I also attended NSCAA Conventions and took my NSCAA Premier Course. In the space of two years, I took advantage of every book, course, and resource I could get my hands on. Now I needed experience to try these methods out for myself.

Soon, I got a fantastic opportunity to put my new ideas into action and I became Head Women's Soccer Coach at Wingate University. I had visions of playing the beautiful game the right way, with passing combinations like Arsenal and Barcelona. I also wanted my players to enjoy the game and have fun with it. The focus of all my work was on everything I had learned, but I had not devised a system on the practice field to connect all my fresh knowledge on the different areas of the game. The consequence of this was that my results were inconsistent. We would win two games and lose one and that was the regular pattern. We had the most talented team in the league, in my opinion, but were finishing in the mid-table. This didn't make sense! Although my training ideas were innovative, my relationships with players could have been a lot better and I found it hard to get my message across during a game using the same motivational methods with each player. Likewise, I could not understand how a change in formation half-way through the second half did not turn the game around in our favor. It worked for Mourinho! I was young and in an environment where I could try different things but I had to find a way to piece the puzzle together. I needed to connect the dots and create a winning culture that would improve my players in every aspect and motivate my players in a system that they could understand and benefit from.

Finding a Philosophy To Fit My Goals

Although Mourinho was a great role model for me as a young, ambitious coach, I got it all wrong when identifying what made him 'special'. I watched the TV interviews, read the newspaper articles, saw the sureness on the bench, and basically believed the hype. He was born with all the answers, winning came easy, and there is no reason why it should not happen to me as well. Boy was I naïve! Upon closer inspection you can clearly see that Mourinho's rise to the top was driven more by perspiration than inspiration. This tenacity, drive, and determination was what I should replicate and channel it into how I could be effective as myself. I did not make a sudden, conscious decision to change a lot of things as a coach, but I did decide that in order for me to reach my goals, I had to 'be better'. It was as simple as that. I had to be more organized. I had to collect as much information about my players as I could, and chart everything. I had to improve my sessions and communicate with equal quality. Lecturing my players on different tactical systems would not cut it anymore. Most importantly, I had to find a way to combine physical, tactical, technical, and mental elements of coaching and learn how to physically prepare my players with periodization, strength and conditioning, and recovery techniques.

On top of everything, I had to *win*. Yes, the beautiful game which I grew up playing with a smile on my face now came with big responsibilities. This shaped my new philosophy more than anything. I developed an edge, a competitiveness that was never there before. In my early years as a coach, I walked off the field too many times thinking that my team had played better but not earned the result. "Today wasn't our day," I was almost happy to tell myself. I learned how to lose but realized that it was in danger of becoming a habit. I was not thinking as a modern coach and this had to change. I made a vow to win every game I played. And it wasn't just words. I wanted to develop an effective system in all areas of the game: tactically, on the practice field, dealing with the physical and mental demands, that would help get my team the result they deserved every week. Nothing was left to chance and I would put everything into making sure every minute I had with my team was productive. I had to move from good to great and get absorbed in the process. It would be a different game from now on and I wanted to become a different coach.

A Changing Game

In the past ten years, the coaching climate in the world has changed dramatically. Society has changed, people have changed, and the beautiful game has changed at an incredible speed. And despite this, I have heard on numerous recent radio shows, from great players of past generations, that the game is still the same as it was twenty, thirty or forty years ago. The Tottenham Hotspur team of the 1960s played the same free flowing football of Barcelona and Matt Busby was using the same methods Pep Guardiola used to devastating effect at Barcelona, but forty years earlier. I agree with this view but only to a certain extent. The game is the same only because the field is the same length and width, the ball is the same size, and the referee's decision is still final. For me, that is where it all ends. I may not have experienced soccer before the 1980's but from studying it, I can tell you one thing: it *has* changed enormously!

Players are more athletic now, technically better, and have more access to full-time coaching than they have ever had. With the role of sports science, players have become bigger, stronger and faster than ever before. Changes in society have seen the role of sports psychology become more important than ever. If a player or team lack the mental components needed to achieve success, they will not last long.

Perhaps the biggest change, though, is the financial rewards of playing soccer. There is so much at stake for young players with both professional and soccer scholarships at a premium. This has added pressure from the sidelines with parents wanting results for their child and supporters not content at their hard earned money going towards the salary of an underperformer.

Don't Forget The Pressure

Not all the changes have benefitted the game as a spectacle. More international and Champions League teams set themselves up to not get beaten, playing a system that rarely moves away from deep, compact defending with one lone striker. Games have become less open and fewer coaches send their teams out to attack and entertain. And why would they? Results today are of vital importance in competitive soccer and rightly so. Without results, coaches cannot validate their methods and systems, regardless of performances. Players will doubt the system. How can you sell something that is broken?

In the modern game you will not succeed without results for one simple reason: the squad. Soccer has become a squad game with clubs, teams, and programs typically having two quality players for each position (sometimes more if they have the finances). One of the toughest things for coaches to do today is to pick the team and leave unhappy, healthy players out of the starting lineup. Those players will accept and respect your decision but only if you get a result. Sure, you may be lucky to work with a group of players who happily accept sitting on the bench every game, but they may lack the competitive mentality that drives winners. Top players will be annoyed they are not in your starting line-up and only winning will validate your decision.

With the added pressure to win games and a modern society that has information about every team at every level, coaching can become a very stressful job. And by job, I don't mean full time or lucrative one. Every grass roots level coach is just as likely to feel that pressure. We cannot change pressure but we must deal with it. And we deal with it by getting down to work. It is the aim of this book to make your job easier by constantly looking for ways to improve every aspect of your work as a coach. So let's get started!

Modern Day Coaches

It is no coincidence that the coaches who have adapted their methodology to the modern game, are the most successful ones. José Mourinho, Pep Guardiola, Brendan Rodgers, Andres Villa Boas, and Jürgen Klopp are all coaches who have embraced the modern game and used advanced training techniques on the training ground to take their team to the next level. Mix this with an astute appreciation of tactics and player management and you have a winning combination. Why do I define them as modern coaches? Simple. Their methods are not a secret. Anyone can see how they work by their behaviour on the sidelines, on the practice field, and the way they talk to the media.

They are certainly not one dimensional coaches; they rely on every aspect of their work rather than one intricate drill or system of play. Modern day coaches have a holistic approach to the game. They are tacticians, trainers, fitness fanatics, psychologists, and sometimes a counsellor!

Modern day coaches are just as impressive off the field as they are on it. They are great communicators, innovators, and show strong emotional control when working with their respective teams. Successful coaches today do not possess more knowledge or have different views than their predecessors, but they have realized that their work has to stretch from the game to the practice field, to the weight room, right to the mind of their players. It is a tough task but not an impossible one.

These coaches may be fortunate to work with the best players in the world but they have earned the right to do so. They have reached the top with hard work and smart thinking, alongside an ability to perform under pressure and take calculated risks. If you do the same, exciting things will start to happen. Success in soccer does not care who you are but in order for you to find it, you have to go looking for it!

Setting Ourselves Up For Success

This book is about embracing every aspect of modern day coaching and learning how the various strands intertwine. Yes, tactics are important, but not if your players are not fit enough to press and cover ground. In the same way, a midfielder with great technique will not be effective if he or she cannot make quick decisions. It is all connected. Every factor has an effect on the game and the foundation must be set on the practice field. As coaches, we must lead the way. If you as a coach cannot change and evolve, you will get left behind. Tactical systems have become complicated and players have more questions. The way you communicate these answers to the players is more important than the answer themselves.

In this book, we will look at the problems that coaches face today, and the solutions they can implement to get the most out of their team. From training methods, to systems of play, to ways of getting the best out of your players and out of yourself. Winning is not guaranteed. It never is in soccer. Your team always steps on the field with a possibility of a win, loss, or a tie. But I will guarantee this: your team will become better in every aspect of the game, you will become better as a coach, your players will enjoy playing for you, and you will significantly increase your chances of winning.

Success leaves clues and this book will give you a number of important pointers that you will require to be successful in the game today. Modern coaches are moving forward in the game at alarming speed. They are well organized, they understand their players and their players want to play for them. Modern coaches do not cling to excuses as a defense mechanism for a defeat or a poor performance.

Chapter 1

So how do you become a modern coach? If you are reading this book -
you are already on the way. You hold the key to your team's success by
your thinking and through your work. Working smart is almost as
important as working hard. Your players need you to be outstanding in
every area of the game and you owe it to them to be better every time
they work with you. The effect of your modern approach will be
phenomenal; just wait to see the reaction of your players and watch them
follow suit. You are bright, enthusiastic, confident, and ready to help them
deal effectively with everything the game has to throw at them. Who
wouldn't want to play for a coach like that!? So let's waste no time and get
to work!

2

The Game Is Moving But Where Are The Coaches?

Ask one hundred coaches how the game is changing and the majority will answer with "The players are getting stronger and faster". Although correct, this is an inadequate answer as it is too general a view of the modernization of soccer. So general, in fact, that it sounds like everything is out of the coaches' hands. Instead, we must look deeper at the game and not only see where the changes are occurring, but also find solutions and ways to adapt our methods accordingly.

As a coach, it can be easy to become consumed in our work and find ourselves missing the groundbreaking changes in the game today. And whilst some coaches do recognize and take notice of them, the majority will not re-evaluate their methods to adapt to them. Coaches are creatures of habit and time moves fast. This can be a dangerous combination. What worked for one group of players may not work for another; likewise what worked in one era, will almost certainly fail in the next.

The greatest coaches evolve over time so awareness of the game has to be in your makeup. In the 1970s, FIFA "Coach of the Century" Rinus Michels developed a unique philosophy called 'Total Football' with his Dutch team. It was the purist form of soccer: free flowing, entertaining, an attacking style, and high pressure defensively. It was poetry in motion for a soccer coach. Coaches had found the answer and the standard was set. But would those ideas work in the game today? Yes, Michels' principles of movement and 'team first' ethos are still outstanding, but the techniques that we use to instill them into our players have to change and develop. Why should we look to modernize Rinus Michel's ideas and theories? Let's take a closer look at the areas of change in recent years.

Role of Goalkeepers

The days when goalkeepers used to stand between the posts, save a couple of shots, and simply kick a few balls as long as they could are long gone! The evolution of goalkeeping has transformed the game in recent years. Modern goalkeepers are just as good with their feet as some of their fellow midfielders. A top keeper today will be met with blank stares from his teammates if he/she fails to deal effectively with a tricky backpass. This has led to attacks starting further down the field and as the technical demands for keepers has increased, so too has the tempo of the game. Forwards chase backpasses now to simply affect the service from the goalkeeper, knowing that a keeper with time on the ball can usually place a ball wherever they want to. Physical conditioning of goalkeepers has changed drastically also. Can you imagine Manuel Neuer struggling during preseason testing at Bayern Munich? Goalkeepers now operate with the same fitness and technical standards as outfield players. The psychological stress of being a goalkeeper in the modern game has also changed significantly. You only have to look at Joe Hart to see how errors become national news in the build-up to England games.

Deep Playmaker

I grew up in an era where the playmaker was a center midfielder or withdrawn forward who could influence the game high up the field with a range of assists or goals. Dennis Bergkamp, Gianfranco Zola, Roberto Baggio, Eric Cantona, and Lothar Matthäus are just a few examples of such great players who captured the imagination of the 1990s. This type of player has changed significantly in recent years as stifling defenses and rigid defensive systems have drawn them further down the field.

The dangerous playmaker has been replaced by a deep lying string puller, able to impact a game by changing the point of attack: retaining possession, and controlling the tempo. This type of player has developed from what was a novelty ten years ago into a necessity in top level soccer today. Busquets, Pirlo, Alonso, Schweinsteiger, Carrick, and Gundogan are all the first name on the team sheets for their respective Champions League teams and coaches now have to think of how to stop these players from dictating the play against their teams. If you think they are less dangerous than the attacking playmakers, watch just how effective they can be if they are allowed to play without pressure!

Playmaking Center Backs

Who would have thought twenty years ago that 'range of passing' would be one of the most important attributes for a central defender? For some top level teams, it has even become the priority. As more teams drop deep to defend with ten players and play counter-attacking soccer, this has allowed defenders more time on the ball and the freedom to make decisions on how to construct an attack. Central defenders must now be excellent technically as well as for other aspects of the game. I remember Rudd Gullit being introduced to the Premier League in 1995 and no one could believe that this 'libero' type player could be used throughout a season. Today it is the norm. Barcelona defender, Gerald Pique drives through into the opposition half easily a dozen times in a game. If your center back can carry the ball into the opposition half, it can open a range of attacking options for your team. Likewise, if your center back is not comfortable in possession, you will find yourself under an enormous amount of pressure.

Decline of Fixed Systems of Play

The days of rigid tactics and formations are well and truly gone in the modern era. A team, today, competing at a high level could play against a different system every week. Each game will bring different questions, both offensively and defensively. If you are reliant on one system your players will be limited in their ability to solve problems as they arise on the field. Systems of play trend just as much as the success of different teams, in fact it could be said that they trend at the same rate. As the soccer landscape changes, there are no longer revolutionary breakthroughs in tactics. As players have developed into better athletes and improved technically, it has brought formations closer together and they have become very similar. So similar, in fact, that a 4-5-1 can become a 4-4-2 or a 4-3-3 within seconds. Teams have different defensive and offensive formations and for some, like Spain in Euro 2012, it can simply become a philosophy. How could an attack minded coach send their team out to play without a recognized center forward ten or fifteen years ago? Croatia Head Coach Slaven Bilic summed it up perfectly when he said, "Systems are dying – it's about the movement of ten players now." Tactically now, in the modern game, your players will have multiple roles within the attacking and defensive framework.

Psychological Profile of Players

There has been a huge psychological change in players in recent years. This is evident across the world and has left a lot of coaches scratching their heads and struggling to adapt. The days of coaches relying solely on authoritarian methods reaching high levels of success are well and truly gone. Try asking your players to run laps to warm-up or do hill runs for fitness. You will be greeted with blank looks. Demotivation in action! Instead, players today have to know *why* they are doing something, and some are reluctant to do extra away from the practice field. Individual training has become a lost art, and you will rarely see a player arrive early or stay behind to work by themselves to improve their game. We also now have a 'YouTube' generation who watch goals instead of games and 30 second clips have replaced Match Of The Day.

Changes in attention span throughout society can also impact upon the soccer world; a coach who overelaborates on a technical point is now "lecturing" players and a coach who adds thirty minutes of fitness work at the end of a session is now a "slavedriver". Both may seem harsh but they have the same effect, the players will not buy into these training methods any more. The modern coach will have to reduce 'practice boredom' during sessions as well as challenging and pushing all players. Today the players will challenge you as much as you challenge them so you must be adaptable and fully equipped to deal with it.

Has the Role of the Coach Changed?

The days of the old school manager whose sole responsibility was to pick the team and give a rousing speech before the match and during half time have now well and truly faded away. Perfect examples are former Nottingham Forest players turned coaches, Martin O'Neill and Roy Keane, who both tried to copy the management techniques of legendary Brian Clough by staying away from the training ground in midweek and saving their impact for games. This tactic failed miserably for both men. Players need day to day interactions with their coaches.

Old school coaches have been replaced by those who work tirelessly throughout the week on the practice field on team shape and movement, in preparation for game day. With so many changes in the game, a modern coach is required to be a counselor, psychologist, scientist, and master tactician. Yes, the demands on modern day coaches can be overwhelming; more pressure to win, more types of problems to deal with, more games to play, more scrutiny of methods, and demands to give players undivided attention, has meant that coaches have had to evolve. In order for coaches to be successful in the modern era, they must be aware of these changes and learn how to deal with them.

The Pitfalls of Traditional Coaching

As a coach myself, I have the utmost respect for all coaches, regardless of age, generation, or level. When you stand on the sideline you join a group of people who give the game a part of themselves but are always at the mercy of results and criticism. You don't know what is going on within their team, but you know exactly what they are going through. However, as I have studied training techniques and observed sessions throughout the years, I have seen traditional methods of coaching, still very common today, that can slow down and even block the progress of players and teams alike.

Too Many are Results Focused

With so much pressure to get results today, it is understandable that coaches get carried away by the final result. Yes, it is important and one of the main reasons why we play - I completely agree - but the result must not consume the coach. The performance must also be the priority of the coach – this is key!

Focus on results over performance and you will stop doing the things necessary to deliver a victory in the first place. Focus on performance over results and you will always have a *reason* why you won or did not win the game. If your team delivers a great performance, your chance of winning goes up to 70%. Sometimes you will win a game in which you underperform, and sometimes you will lose a game in which your team was fantastic. That is part of the game. Coaches who focus on the results alone will wonder why their team loses four games in a row. Keep emotional control and your team will also.

Let's NOT Take It One Game at a Time

The old phrase in soccer "We'll take it one game at a time" could be the most misleading phrase in the history of the game. Yes, from a psychological point of view you certainly should only focus on one task at a time and never look too far ahead. However, it is vital that as a coach, you do not take this approach to how you view your season. No matter what country, or level of soccer you play in the world, the awards are given out at the end of the season. Great coaches work from the end backwards. This means that you have to peak at the right time in order to be in a position to win at the right time.

By taking it one game at a time and not planning efficiently, coaches fail to take the physical and performance function into account throughout the season. Patterns happen but you have to look for them and expect them. Sir Alex Ferguson would give Cristiano Ronaldo two weeks off at Christmas every season. Did United need him? Of course! With fixture congestion and crucial points at stake, Ronaldo was needed in every game. But looking at how to manage Ronaldo physically was in the mind of Sir Alex. Of course it paid off and this is just one great example of how we, as coaches, have to look at the season. A coach who expects his forward to function with the same quality during the first week of the season as the last, without a long term plan in place, will be very fortunate if this works out at the end of the season.

What Works for One DOES NOT Work for All

You cannot train all players to have the exact same skills set when the game will demand the opposite. This means that having defenders, midfielders, and forwards, all working on the same principles for each session will hold more players back than will progress them. This is where your training has to be functional and specialized.

Players need to be working on whatever skills set they will have to be performing in a game instead of utilizing the coach's session plan. Manchester United legend Ole Gunnar Solskjær used to score over 100 goals a week in competitive practice sessions. Did teammate Roy Keane do the same? Absolutely not, because training at United was structured so that Solskjær had opportunities to rehearse his strengths, the same way Keane did.

Players have different needs and your sessions must recognize this. Put your players in positions they will have to perform in games. The challenge of modern coaching is to have practice sessions that incorporates the demands required for *each* player and their respective positions. All practice must replicate game stimuli. If players fail to recognize the correct stimuli when it is demanded in a game, technique and skill execution will fail. It is the responsibility of the coach to make sure this does not happen.

The One Dimensional Model Of Coaching

Before soccer changed in recent years, training programs have largely been, and still are in many cases, one dimensional.

In the traditional training program, only one aspect of the game is worked on at any one time, or over any one session. For example, if improving fitness is the goal for the coach, he will leave the balls in the bag and devise a complex cross country route around the field or even offsite. Then if a coach wants to improve a technical aspect of the game, we typically see players partnered up five yards apart - passing and working on controlling the ball five yards apart in a stationary position. The benefits of this type of training are limited. The players cannot transfer this activity to a game-like situation because it is rare that a player will receive the ball five yards away from him/her, control it, and pass it right back ten times in a row. What is more - speed, intelligence, and fitness levels are not tested and the player is under no pressure from time or opposition.

This one dimensional training program is counterproductive for a number of reasons:

- Mentally, it does not stimulate top players. You are not testing their ability to perform difficult tasks so therefore it is not challenging them. For this reason, players consider it 'boring'.

- It is unrealistic to the modern game.

- It is impossible to develop a 'thinking' player; one who can solve problems during the game without constant direction from a coach.

- It does not prepare players for the physical demands of a game.

- Players' habits become "one and done". After performing an action or skill in a game, the player usually is unsure of the next move and consequently stands still.

- Tempo is typically low for these sessions.

Movement patterns are very limited. Players become static and easy to play against. The movement of forward players in youth soccer today, when the ball is not within 20 yards of them, is a great example of this. One dimensional exercise means that players are under coached in too many areas. How many times do we evaluate players and they have glaring weaknesses in physicality, skill, or game intelligence? This is because their training program has been one dimensional during their development years.

Is Your Training Model One Dimensional?

Many coaches have one dimensional training models but fail to notice. By simply asking yourself these questions, you can tell whether or not your training program is one dimensional:

- Do you separate your sessions for technical, tactical and physical conditioning?

- Do your players continually struggle with the tactical aspects of the game?

- Do your players continually struggle to create chances?

- Does your team continually start the game sluggish?

- Does your team have a problem conceding goals in the last ten minutes of games?

- Is attendance a continual problem for your training sessions?

- Do players continually feel like they can sit out of a session and not miss anything?

- Is enthusiasm from your players continually missing during your training sessions?

The word 'continually' is mentioned in every question because that means that your team has developed a *habit* of doing something. Aristotle once famously said, "We are what we repeatedly do, therefore excellence is not an act but a habit." The same is true for soccer teams, except you only have to look at the practice field to see where these habits are made. No matter how many times a coach shouts instructions during a game, a player will always resort back to his/her habits because habit will always be stronger than reason.

If you answered yes for any of the questions above it does not make you a bad coach! Every coach, including the top ones, have problems to fix on a daily basis, it is the nature of the game. However, too many times we believe that these problems are because of the *deficiencies of our players* and not down to the habits we help create every day. You can fix these problems on the practice field but it is important to understand that you, the coach, are ultimately responsible for creating an environment where your players can develop winning habits every day.

The last question was a very important one. Enthusiasm is a regular visitor to any successful sports practice facility. Players arrive early, the atmosphere is always good, laughter can always be heard when players are interacting with each other as they meet. This is the perfect environment for teams and players to get better because everyone wants to be there. If they are happy and ready to go out and practice, you have a healthy culture in your program. Practice should be a 'fun' place to be. Of course, there is also a time to focus and concentrate, so it is important that the team realizes this and your job as a coach will be educating the players on which is which.

Summary

The average soccer player today has 3000 changes of direction per game. Many of those changes will involve the ball and other stimuli on the field for the player to process and make decisions upon. And they have to do those actions at full speed with pressure from coaches, fans, and themselves. In a nutshell, those are the demands on the modern soccer player. Not easy is it!?

Now, how does running laps and standing stationary across from a partner for long periods of time prepare the player for these challenges? Quite simply, it doesn't. It may work on technique and concentration but it misses out on more important aspects that actually benefit players, and which are relevant to the game. When you work at higher levels, your training methodology should advance along with the quality of players. Late Wales National Team Head Coach Gary Speed warned coaches who refuse to change the way they work that "If you're not careful, the players recognize that you are using outdated methods because they have been with other clubs and have used different methods. So you will lose credibility amongst your players."

Imagine that the game you have played and coached your whole life one day leaves you behind? You cannot connect with your players as easily as you once did. Performances are flat, training sessions become stagnant, and you cannot seem to have any effect on either. It can easily happen. In fact, it is happening to thousands of coaches right at this time. Your goal is to make sure it does not happen to you. And there is only one solution; you have to change your training methodology and how you work on the practice field. Quite simply, you cannot consider yourself a modern coach if you do not prepare your players for the modern game. In the next chapter we will turn common sense into common practice as we look to not only connect with our players, but inspire them to transfer the quality from the practice field, to the match itself.

3

The Answer

When Manchester City fired Roberto Mancini in the summer of 2013, the club owners announced that they wanted to "develop a holistic approach to all aspects of football at the club". The club demanded a coach who has good relationships with players, staff, and directors, and who could excel as a leader for the club as a brand, on and off the field. Fans scratched their heads – Mancini is a world class coach who delivered the first Premiership title to the team only 12 months before. But get used to it folks because every club in the world, whether it is professional, amateur, youth, or college program, is turning into a version of Manchester City.

Winning is not enough to be successful in coaching soccer anymore. Parents, fans, shareholders, whoever it is, want to know exactly what is going on inside your team. Social media, fan sites, and forums have turned even youth teams into this pressure cooker model for a club. There used to be a closed doors policy that existed amongst coaches and their teams. The practice field was a sanctuary for the coach, a shelter from criticism and a way to push your players to their limits without worrying about outside interference.

Coaches today are under as much scrutiny off the practice field as they are on it. You can no longer coach in the dark, keeping your ideas and methods close to your chest. Everyone now wants to know all about you. So how will you adapt as a coach? Successful coaches will thrive under this global change in the soccer landscape because they will use it to their advantage. It is an opportunity to analyze every part of your efforts. Your work will now have to be bulletproof in order to be successful. Therefore, if you are going to be questioned and interrogated on your coaching methods, you better be prepared to back it up with quality planning and implementation. So let's rid ourselves of the "this is the way it has always been done" attitude and get to work!

The "What" of Modern Coaching

If there is an easy part of coaching, it has to be what ideas and philosophies we want our teams to incorporate. These will vary from coach to coach but tend to cover general ideals such as high work rate, possession focused, attack minded, defensively solid, high tempo, etc. There is no right or wrong answer and this is the very much the theory side of coaching. It can be a set of ideals that you will stand by no matter what. For example, Roberto Martinez brings the same fluid passing style to each of his clubs. Or the coach can adapt his what depending on the players he has in his squad or the demands of the league. A good example of a coach who does this is Carlo Ancelotti, who has various systems and philosophies; his Juventus, Chelsea, Paris St. Germain, and Real Madrid teams have all been set up very differently. However, simply identifying your philosophies and being prepared to stand by them is not enough in the game today. Whilst traditional coaching very much consisted of ordering and telling - today's coaching is about nurturing and enhancing, so we need to take a step further.

The "How" of Modern Coaching

This is where coaching becomes more complex and tricky. How can we get our philosophy and ideas through to the players in order to deliver performances and results? A coach and his players can sometimes seem miles apart. The screaming from the sidelines met with a blank expression from your player is a prime example of this in action. It is a long way from the "What" to the "How" and you will need a bridge to get there. Your bridge must be stable and strong - otherwise it will look like the famous rope bridge in the Indiana Jones movie!

The foundations of the bridge will determine your success; your training program makes up the four beams on the bridge: technical, tactical, physical, and mental.

These are the elements that have to be included in every aspect of your work and your goal is to have your team operating as efficiently as possible. If you implement your training program with high standards, consistency, and quality control, you and your team will start moving forward very quickly. So let's make sure that bridge is strong and ready to go.

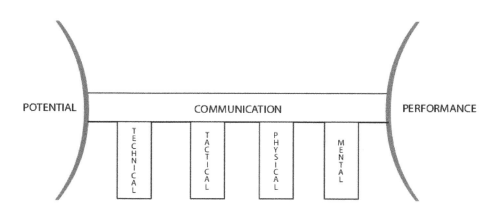

Four Dimensional Coaching

When you use the bridge model, you are now practising "Four Dimensional Coaching", integrating technical, tactical, physical, and mental elements in each part of your practice along with effective communication throughout. We have already discussed how working on each separate beam in isolation is unrealistic to the game. Soccer is inherently a high intensity, multi skilled, contact sport with a lot going on at the same time. It is certainly not a narrow activity or a closed skill so it is vital we prepare for the different variables that it brings.

Technical

Technical proficiency is the ability to perform underlying techniques accurately, consistently, and at game speed. The best teams execute the basics correctly and do it often. Your role as a coach is to provide your players with a technical framework in your sessions so that they can meet the technical demands of the game.

Traditional practice programs that focus on short passing one session, shooting the next, and heading the next will not develop effective, competent performers. If we focus on single skill effectiveness, we are turning our players towards a narrow focus of the sport. Rarely will a player be required to just run and pass the ball in straight lines for an entire game. However, if we expose them to all the different skills that they will face in a game, they will transfer those skills and performance levels will increase. Your exercises should therefore incorporate multi-skills (passing, shooting, control, heading) whilst challenging players to do even more. More is not necessarily an increase in the amount of technical work, but rather the creation of challenging conditions around them, most notably the pressure of opposition and speed of play. Examples of this would be to focus on areas like body shape when players receive the ball and how to create a yard of space. Additional stimuli like this for the player to interpret will challenge them further than simply more repetitions. Traditional practices almost always begin with technical work, at which time players are usually fresh mentally and physically. But in reality, fatigue is a factor in performance so we must prepare our players to pass the ball just as well in the last ten minutes of a game as they do in the first. In order to do this, we must create sessions that challenge them across multiple aspects and not solely on skill.

Tactical

Tactical proficiency is the ability to weigh up game situations, decide what option to take, and when to take it. Working on tactical shape and formations typically slows a session down, but putting the emphasis on your principles is different and a lot more effective. These tactical principles such as pressing, dropping deep, or counter attacking will be the basis of your coaching so it is vital that players understand terminology before working on this.

Game situations are at the heart of this method. Working alongside physical and mental components, tactical thinking is important because players will have to make tactical decisions in a very short window of time - speed of thought will be just as vital as physical speed. The balance of training is crucial because if the coach stops and starts the session too much, flow disappears and you have eliminated key challenges that players will be exposed to in a game. Too often, the tactical side of training is geared for outcome and not process. In other words, coaches change formation or game plans so regularly that players never get a chance to develop performance routines. Having a tactical focus will enable players to Read, Respond, React, and Recover to all situations that will occur in a game.

Physical

You need to have physical competence in order to have skill, tactical, or mental competence. They are inextricably linked because the physical component can have a direct impact on technical or tactical execution. In fact, you could argue that physical development should be the most important component of training because if players are fatigued performing a skill, they will not perform it optimally.

But being physically fit must be soccer specific. Louis van Gaal saw physical and tactical components as very much closely related, "Lots of coaches devote their time to wondering how they can ensure that their players are able to do a lot of running during a match. Ajax trains its players to run as little as possible on the field. That is why positional games are always central to Ajax training sessions."

Forget about laps and complex fitness exercises. If you want to get your players at their best physically, you have to incorporate the ball and soccer specific demands to your session. Speed, power, agility, reaction time, and aerobic endurance that can be sustained for 90 minutes are required. Identifying those demands is one thing, but the key is to integrate these components with game specific indicators during practice sessions. Performance is a function of fitness and fatigue and players must have the energy systems required to meet these demands.

Mental

Psychological proficiency in soccer involves choosing and maintaining a positive attitude, dealing effectively with teammates, using positive self-talk, understanding mental imagery, managing anxiety effectively, developing confidence, controlling emotions effectively, and maintaining concentration. Every session should challenge players in a number of these areas.

A coach who understands sports psychology will be able to unlock the mental doors that each player has in order to reach optimal performance. Perhaps the most important mental aspect will be decision making. Can your exercises challenge players to think and solve problems? This is where the mental component meets the tactical one. A great example is when legendary Chicago Bulls Head Coach Phil Jackson had a "no timeout" policy when his Chicago Bulls team were struggling. It gave his players the responsibility to solve the problems they were facing. His star player, Michael Jordan believed that the team subsequently developed "think power" which would allow them to deal with problems as they occurred throughout the season. Players must be taught how to think, not necessarily what to think. Challenges will occur throughout their lives, on and off the field, so you must prepare them for how to deal with that.

Communication

Your work does not end once you organize and prepare a session. That is just the beginning. You have to drive the session with effective communication and make sure that the tempo remains high and players understand their roles throughout. Driving the tempo means having enthusiasm and high energy levels that players can feed off. You also have to be positive especially when the players' gusto levels start to drop because that is when they need you. Players do not get inspired by "fault finders" and instead need to be rewarded for their work.

We all had a coach when we were younger who continually stopped the practice to pinpoint mistakes and highlight negatives. Frustration eventually takes over our desire to learn. Coaches should look for successful cues from players on every occasion. Finding the good things that our players do is helpful in two ways: firstly, you are strengthening their habits and are guaranteed to see more quality if you acknowledge them at every opportunity. Secondly, you do not need to stop the session to do so. Your positive feedback throughout a session will instead inspire players to do more. A positive attitude is contagious on the practice field and players love it when their coach is excited about what they are doing. We will discuss the role of communication as a coach further in Chapter 10.

The "Why" of Modern Coaching

As well as having training methods that can be easily transferred to the demands of the game, one of the biggest benefits of implementing a consistent four dimensional approach to your practice will be a healthy environment for your players. Because they know practice will be high tempo and enjoyable, they will arrive early and bring a passion for practicing, which will provide a lift to everyone in your program. This makes your training program unique and differentiates you amongst your competition.

Do you know how many training sessions get off on the wrong foot before the session even starts because of the players' perceptions of what lies ahead? I would say a lot of them! Players will be engaged when they work with you because they will have no other option. Your exercises will make them think, it will make them move constantly, and the physical demands on them will mean that when they get recovery breaks, they will use them exactly for that.

When players are being challenged in all aspects of the game, they know you are helping them improve. After practice, even after a tough session, players will want to come back and see what you have in store for them tomorrow. They subconsciously trust you to make them better and therefore become more open to your ideas and philosophies, which will be crucial throughout the seasons when tough decisions have to be made. It may not sound groundbreaking but if you create an atmosphere within your training program that people want to be a part of, you will draw so much positive energy from your players.

Balance

How you balance all four components of training is up to you and the level of your players. It may also depend on the time of year. Pre-season would see an overload on the physical and technical demands whereas the final weeks would see tactics and mental side of games being stressed so that you have a strong finish. Either way, balance is the key and you have to make sure you understand where your team requires the most help. Players can be physically great but if they lack the technical capacity to pass the ball ten yards, then you will not reach peak performance.

If you continue to neglect either technical, tactical, physical, or mental components you may still be successful, but your players will not operate at an optimal level. They rely on each other. You must have the physical competence to do the technical work. You must have technical competence to do the tactical work. And you need mental competences like concentration, focus, emotional control, and decision making skills with you all the way. Too much of one component can also be dangerous. For example, an overemphasis on technique typically leads to frustration for coaches as we wonder why exercises and drills break down technically. Then we put more pressure on our players to make sure it doesn't happen again. This becomes counterproductive to your communication as you are creating an atmosphere of fear instead of one that seeks to express skill.

The Right Environment

Our aim as a coach is not to become what our coaches were when we were young. Too many coaches make that mistake and emulate what exercises and drills they did as a young player. As generations change, so should coaching styles. Instead, we should try and develop players who know how to play the game effectively and can do so in a safe, enjoyable environment. There is a big difference between fun and enjoyment. Fun is players laughing and appreciating the time they have with one another. This can happen in any program. Enjoyment, however, occurs when players become competent at playing the game. This is what they need you for! If enjoyment is not a priority in your coaching, then I highly recommend you make it one. If your players enjoy coming to your practice, being challenged, and working hard as individuals and as a team, then you will create a positive soccer environment and this will be reflected in your team's performance on game day.

Going back to Manchester City and Roberto Mancini, we do not have the benefit of seeing how his training program was set up from week to week, but we were often given insights into his communication. Every week in the media there was player unrest and even practice field bust-ups between coaches and players. It does not matter how talented your players are, if your environment is not conducive to players growing and reaching their potential, your position is always at risk.

The Special Way

In the summer of 2012, I was fortunate to spend two days with José Mourinho and Real Madrid at a pre-season camp in Los Angeles with the NSCAA. I was like a kid on Christmas Day. This was my chance to watch and learn from the best in the world. It did not disappoint and was a phenomenal experience, but one of the most striking things about the trip was just how open Jose Mourinho was about his methods and how he works. His staff explained their roles, everyone gave detailed analyses of what their responsibilities were and the key to their success.

Throughout the event, Mourinho was as confident in his delivery as he seems every week in his press conferences. His areas of emphasis were also technical, tactical, physical, and mental. However, the secret to his success was how he connected every aspect of his work together. This was a great example of four dimensional coaching. Mourinho added: attention to detail, high quality control, and an emphasis on positive communication throughout the club, to make his training model first class in every sense. It was modern, it was unique, and the response of the players was on a different level. Mention "pre-season" to any player and they usually break out in a cold sweat, but the Real Madrid players looked like they were having the time of their lives. Experienced professionals like Ronaldo, Alonso, Ramos, and Kaka (many of whom were coming off a strenuous Euro 2012 campaign) were out thirty minutes before the session started and even after a tough session, stayed behind thirty minutes longer to do extra work on their own. I left with an appreciation that it was not Mourinho's philosophy or his media interviews that is the key to his success, but rather his "bridge" and how he goes about connecting the dots that sets him apart.

Summary

Every day we are supplied with more evidence of how the game is changing. A group of Australian researchers recently analyzed the World Cup Finals from 1966 through to 2010. They found that ball speed had increased by about 15%, the density of players around the ball had increased, and the number of passes attempted per minute had increased by a phenomenal 35%.

Players are covering more ground, playing quicker, and faster, so is that a physical, technical, tactical, or mental change? The answer is simple: every component is involved. If you do not have a four dimensional approach to your training program, you may get to the top of the ladder but then realize it was leaning against the wrong building. In other words, you may experience short term success but will eventually reach a level of competition and your team will come up short. There is always a higher level and when you play those teams, they will be better prepared and they will win.

Remember, knowledge does not become power until it is used. Any coach can come up with a "What". Planning and developing the "How" and the "Why" will differentiate you and take you to another level. But it is not easy. If a fan, parent, or even a player asks why you are doing something a certain way, you should have a calm and well prepared answer because of your planning. Instead of driving to a practice and thinking of what you will do, you will have prepared for it in a professional manner and know that every minute is vital. You will have to put more time and energy into your coaching but you will be rewarded for doing so. Your players will see your intensity and your practices will mean as much as the game itself.

Chapter 3

The "What" involves words but the "How" and "Why" takes action and hard work. We have used the bridge and are well on the road to success. There are even more complex ways to personalize your work as we find out that coaching is not a "one size fits all" business.

4

The Non-Negotiables

As much as we can learn from the likes of José Mourinho, David Moyes, Brendan Rodgers and Arrigo Sacchi – copying isolated training exercises alone will not work. Coaches regularly receive emails from programs offering us "How To Play Like Barcelona" and "Play the Brazilian Way" with success guaranteed within a short period of time, but it is never that simple. There is no 'One-Size-Fits-All' or 'Quick Fix' method for success; otherwise we would all be using it! Instead of simply looking at replicating a high profile coach, we need to look closer to home for answers.

Your players will tell you what they need, and don't need, in your sessions. This is apparent by seeing what areas they struggle in, and how effective they are at certain times or areas of the pitch. No team is the same. We all operate at different levels, different age groups, different levels of expectations, different climates, and different cultures where the training program will have to be adjusted accordingly. There are, however, certain training principles that cannot be compromised in order for your team to adapt to the modern game. In my observation of training methods over the past ten years, these factors have been the difference between good sessions and great sessions. If you keep these principles fixed within in your sessions, you will be on your way to creating a unique, winning, modern training environment.

Push The Tempo!

Training exercises in Serie A, La Liga, Bundesliga, or Dutch Eredivisie are all different but the top teams share one common theme in the sessions: Tempo. A high tempo practice is when players perform EVERY activity at full speed. Working at a higher intensity will improve your players as they are forced to concentrate and solve problems and are tested, both technically and tactically, at full speed.

When tempo is high on your list of goals for each session, your exercises should provide an overload for your players to perform and maintain as many explosive actions as possible. Too often coaches wait for the players to dictate whether the session tempo will be high. This attitude will ensure that your team will always struggle with a high paced game and come up short at the end of games due to lack of fitness and fatigue. Not only should you walk on the practice field and demand tempo from day one, but you should never accept it when it drops from your players or your team.

If an exercise demands the player to make a supporting run, pressure another player, or transition from attack to defense, it should be performed at maximum speed and effort. And if they are walking or even jogging when they should be performing high intensity exercises, then you must address it during the session, rather than ignore it and watch it happen in a game.

It is not always natural for players to train this way because it involves them stepping outside their comfort zone, and they may prefer to reserve full intensity for games. You must stress that 'how you practice is how you play' and overcome any resistance through your organization and ability to coach. There are a number of 'tempo zappers' that you should be aware of in your practice sessions. Look out for these:

- Long Lines – Exercises that have more than four players waiting to perform an activity means that they have too much time to switch off mentally and drop their intensity levels.

- Lectures – Feedback is vital for the success of a session, but if you stop the play every five minutes to talk in great detail, the pace of your session will drop very quickly. Remember how frustrated you get when the referee continually stops the game for infringements? The players feel the same way when the coach turns practice into a sermon.

- Disorganized Practice – The session should flow in more ways than one. If players have to wait five minutes in the middle of the session for the coach to set up the next exercise, the intensity of the session will drop significantly. Get there early and set up your whole practice. Keep the breaks short and for recovery only, that way the players will learn how to refocus quickly and often.

- Punishments – If players do not achieve the desired outcome in any part of the exercises, penalizing them can be detrimental to the flow of the session. There is nothing wrong with addressing failure with your players before or after the practice. In the middle of a practice however, it can have adverse effects. Taking a negative approach within certain stages of the session may work from time to time, but if they become a regular occurrence you will soon find your players playing conservatively, looking to minimize mistakes and that will disrupt the tempo. For example, a defensive player may opt against an overlapping run if they feel that the consequence of the move breaking down is too great. Negative energy and negative thoughts will block positive thoughts and creative thoughts from occurring. We never want to take the power of positivity away from our sessions.

Use the Clock!

Your management of time is a crucial factor in determining the quality of a training session. A stopwatch can be a coach's greatest ally or biggest threat when aiming to create a high tempo environment at practice. No, we are not looking to stand on a finish line shouting times at our players as they run past. Instead we are creating game-like situations and challenges for our players that must be completed in order to succeed. Lots of coaches arrive at training sessions with excellent session plans complete with game-realistic, challenging exercises for their players. However, the time management of the coach does not maximize the work load of the players and the session falls short of its potential.

Time is traditionally used in training sessions like it is during school. Typically after 30 minutes, the coach moves on to one activity, then after another 30 minutes they move onto the next activity, and so on. There is a certain inevitability about how a session develops and it causes players to stay within their comfort zones.

We should be using the clock to challenge and stimulate our players' thinking, instead of as a guideline to how close they are to being finished. One important thing to realize is that the nature of your timekeeping will dictate the intensity of your session. For example, allowing any exercise to continue over 15 minutes without a stoppage will see the tempo drop very quickly. Players will start performing less dynamic actions and the quality of the game will also drop. Instead, if you try keeping the exercises and games to 3-5 minutes duration, with one minute recovery, and five sets, this then allows players to play at their maximum heart rate for each set and then gradually work on their recovery. The result will be a group of players who are able to work at a higher intensity for longer amounts of time, with shorter periods of rest, which is what the game itself demands.

How long should an effective training session last? Once you get the tempo and intensity up to a high standard, this becomes a key question.

Club practices are typically scheduled for 90 minutes, while it is normal for most college teams to stay out on the practice field for over two hours. In my opinion, this is an area a lot of coaches need to re-evaluate in the modern game. Keeping players out on the practice field for long periods of time, usually leads to a lower tempo and the session mirrors a marathon instead of a game.

Staying out on the practice field for extended time with your team may feel like you are being productive, but can actually cause more harm than good. Plenty of talented teams have left their legs on the practice field, so energy management is hugely important for a coach. There is no correlation between how long you practice and what you accomplish.

Make sure you do not confuse being busy with achieving - being effective with your time is the goal. No matter how good your game plan is, it will never work if your players are tired and lethargic. As a coach, you are responsible for managing the energy levels of your players. Do not waste fatigue on workouts that do not fit the unique needs of your team. An effective coach will taper energy expenditure leading into performance as this correlates highly with having the upper hand at the start of games. Again, you will be rewarded for this approach by your players, with the intensity of your practices and subsequent performances in games.

Practice Variability

Nick Winkelman, a strength and conditioning coach who trains athletes for the NFL combine, recently developed the concept of 'Perfect Practice Versus Practicing Perfectly' which can be used to help how we construct effective training sessions. Most coaches set the goal as 'Perfect Practice' which focuses on the execution of every drill to be as perfect as possible. The aim is to take that perfection and transfer it to the game itself. However, we are aware that there are times when execution in practice can be flawless, but it does not always translate to the game. A more effective way to do this is to 'Practice Perfectly' instead of 'Perfect Practice'. 'Practice Perfectly' centers on the concept of variability, which is how often the coach changes the drill or stimulus that an athlete is exposed to in the context of your training session. For example, let's take three technical skills – passing, heading, and shooting. Low variability practice is doing thirty minutes of basic passing exercises, followed by thirty minutes of basic heading exercises, followed by thirty minutes of basic shooting exercises. High variability, on the other hand, is when you can control and pass, adapt your body shape to perform a header, and then shoot on goal at an angle. By using high variability in your sessions, you are now changing the drill every single repetition. So low variability is doing the same things over again, whereas high variability is more random, just like the demands of a game.

The next development is the idea of 'Contextual Interference' which is the application of practice variability. This is where coaches can take the concept of practice and interfere with it by disrupting accuracy and forcing the player to adapt. When you look at percentage of success when doing 100 basic passes, then 100 headers, and then 100 shots on goal, the chances are that it's going to be quite high. This is because when performing these exercises under repetition, the players get into a groove and benefit from momentum. But what if we now performed those tasks in a randomized order? They may have two shots in a row, one on the right side and one on the left side, before moving to a challenging header, and finishing up with a difficult pass to execute. With this 'High Variability' the chances are the percentage will be lower because of more pressure and less accuracy. So a lower percentage of success in practice is a bad thing right? Not quite. Over 70% of research looking at a wide range of sports has found a "contextual interference effect", which proves that when you have a higher contextual inference and practice is more random, the transfer and retention of learning those skills is superior. Therefore players, can go into games and apply those skills at a higher level rather than simply being successful in practice and struggling in the game. This theory may go against logic because it leads to more failure in practice, but if you want your players to perform in a game, it will be more effective. Of course, young players who are starting the game have to learn the basics before moving towards this type of training but elite players will certainly reap the benefits.

Performance Routines

This is an area of the training program that is often overlooked when aiming to maximize the potential of your team, both individually and collectively. How many players get themselves into positions on the field on game day, only to be taken by surprise? The forward who rushes a shot on goal without realizing they had more time or the goalkeeper who nervously deals with the first back pass are both examples of players who only find themselves in those positions during a game and are visibly uncomfortable. A coach with knowledge of effective performance routines can help his/her players arrive to the game confident and ready for the challenge. Pre-game routines are defined as "A preferred sequence of preparatory thoughts and actions that athletes use in an effort to concentrate effectively before the execution of key skills." (Moran, 2003) A lot of performance routines are psychological, visualizing what will happen during quiet reflection or even having superstitions that help get the mind focused for action. For the most part, players are left to their own devices when it comes to imagery, and as a result, do not use it systematically and fail to see the benefits of it. Coaches often overlook the fact that we can help create these 'pictures' for the benefit of our players. Therefore, we must use our training program to allow players to experience situations that they are going to see in a game and in which they are going to achieve success. By becoming comfortable in game-like situations, the players then learn routines. As the player gets familiar with his/her routines, they then start to see cues which are basically signals to perform a movement at a certain time. The quicker the player sees a cue, the more effective they will be in a game.

We can help our players to develop pre-game performance routines in a number of ways:

- Realistic practices that mirror game situations. Will your forwards have an opportunity to score goals, will your wide players be in positions to deliver service from those key areas, will midfielders get an opportunity to link up the play, and will your defenders and goalkeepers be asked to stop players from scoring in a variety of ways?

- Varied practice exercises so that players will see themselves in as many types of situations as possible.

- Positive individual feedback when you see desired response. Always remember: "What gets recognized gets repeated."

- Clear directions of what is expected in each position. They can be individual written job descriptions for each position or a team template of all positions. The more they are communicated and shared the better, but be careful not to overload each player with too many tasks. Three or four points can be specific enough for a player to digest.

Standards

In order for you to create a consistent, high quality training program you will not only have to identify the standards you are looking for, but you also need to share them with your players as often as possible. High standards allow the coach to have a base for quality control and constantly remind players what will and will not be accepted. Some standards can be very basic: fitness levels required, the warm-up being conducted a certain way, or even how the players dress. When Fabio Capello was coach at AC Milan, all players had to have their socks pulled up throughout practice. Something that may seem so small can have huge effect on self-image of the team and discipline on and off the field. Slightly more complex standards can then make their way to the practice field and can be technique driven, like how the coach wants them to pass the ball, or tactically driven, the importance of defending corners. The more your players are aware of your standards and the more realistic they are to achieve, the more successful you will be at holding your players accountable for their actions. On the practice field, where you will spend the majority of your time interacting with your team, standards are of huge significance because of the message they send to your players. Sir Alex Ferguson once said "As a coach, the one thing you must have is control. You can't afford players to take charge of a training session. There has to be a strong discipline in the training and in general. Simple rules must apply such a time-keeping, concentration at training, etc." Once you identify your standards and share them with your players, it is imperative that you manage them as this will bring consistency to your training program. Make sure your players know that standards do not choose you. If they know the type of tempo that is demanded of them every day in practice and you do not allow players to fall below the expectations, the chances of seeing this level of performance every day increases.

Summary

A traditional coach whose training program lacks the 'Non-Negotiables' and plays against a team of equal or higher ability, will no doubt see his team underperform and most likely lose. The response from the coach is quite common and we hear it often: "I just don't get it. We had a great week of practice and then we played awful." The coach felt that the players only made a few errors in the practice sessions and therefore believed the week's preparation was effective. Keen to avenge the result, the same coach will go back to the practice field following that poor performance and typically change two things: his/her demeanor and the duration of the session. The players will mirror the negative body language they see from their coach and training becomes long, tedious, and consequently counter-productive. All in all, it is a circle of life in soccer that leads to underperformance, player burnout, and minimal progress both as a team and as individuals.

A modern coach on the other hand, manages process, time, and energy in his/her training sessions and, as a result, will see immediate progress and increased probability of success. You are choosing to make practice difficult but rewarding if you create a variable practice program along with a high tempo. In a challenging environment, the players are going to make a lot of mistakes, and the quicker you realize that and accept it, you can then spend your time and energy helping them. Study your players in a game and see how you can help prepare them to be effective in practice. Can your exercises incorporate multiple skills, challenging players in different areas and positions? If so, your players will arrive at the game confident and ready for whatever challenges will come their way. You are preparing them to perform to their maximum potential and they will embrace the responsibility you are giving them with your high standards. You have now left the traditional coach well and truly behind. Now we must look at our training exercises and make sure they are consistent with our standards and beliefs. Let's keep on improving our players and continue to take our training to the next level.

5

Start As You Mean To Continue

The motivational pre-game speech which is used by coaches from around the world, in a wide variety of sports and across eras, has one key objective: to start the game as fast and as positively as possible.

Enter any soccer locker room ten minutes before kick-off and you will hear the same emotional messages. We have all been brought up with an almost identical approach to begin on the front foot and 'set the tone' early. The team that starts quickly can dictate the tempo of the game, gain momentum and confidence, both collectively and individually. However, with that in mind, why is it that our training sessions usually start with slow low-intensity activities creating minimum demands on the players physically, technically, tactically, or psychologically?

The emotional message will not work every day of the week. The more players hear it, the less impact it will generally make. Eventually they will tune it out. Instead, the environment we create needs to teach our players how to start the game the right way. If our training sessions do not mirror the game in every way possible, we are putting ourselves at a disadvantage every time we train and even worse, practice may become irrelevant. With a leisurely and relaxed start to our practices, we then find ourselves constantly playing catch up as players look like they lack impetus and motivation. *We are what we repeatedly do* and we shape our players' training habits every time they step on the practice field. It is vital therefore, that the opening of our session sets us up for success.

Programming your team mentally and physically towards starting both practice and games with purpose and intensity is a valuable skill for a coach. How many times do you see a game where a team who are losing "Go for it" in the last twenty minutes? They take more risks, commit numbers forward, and pressure the ball in all areas of the field with a real urgency. So many times, the late rush comes up short and the losing team effort becomes a case of too little too late.

Instead of bemoaning luck or time, we should instead look at why they chose to start the game on the back foot, waiting to see what their opponents did before they chose to react and become aggressive. The emotional message pre-game talk will always be overruled by habits. These habits are formed on the practice field and too often, set players up for failure in the opening minutes of a game. It is therefore vital that we look at what we do at the beginning of our practice. In the 2011/2012 Premier League season, when the home team scored first, they won the game 71% of the time. With so many foreign coaches in the league, I would argue that the emotional pre-game team talk is not driving this statistic. Instead it is the product of a training environment instilled by the coaches.

The Traditional Warm-Up!

When I was a young player, like many other coaches today, I remember warming-up by running laps of the field. It was like a chore before you were given the privilege of actually playing the game. There was no ball, no mental stimulus, and certainly no tactical link to the game. This method was widely accepted simply because the activity led to increased heart rate.

Following our jog we did static stretching for ten minutes, causing our heart rate to return to its starting point, and thereby negating the effect of the first part of our warm-up. As the session moved towards technical work, there was no intensity as players could pace themselves at their own comfort levels. The end of the session usually meant a game – to the relief of all the players! However, after a sloppy start, because of our half-hearted work rate up to that stage of practice, we typically all reached our maximum heart rate just after the coach yelled, "Next goal wins!" It was a familiar feeling as we all walked off the practice field wishing the games lasted a little longer.

The game has evolved since I was a young player, but one thing has not changed: players want to play as soon as possible. It excites them, it stimulates their minds, and they are almost impossible to distract when a game is in full flow. So why are coaches reluctant to go straight into games? Why hold it above the players as a prize for working hard throughout the session?

Many coaches like to ease their way into training, focusing on perfecting technique and skill execution. For young players this sometimes is a necessity because skills must be honed before you can talk tactics and learn how to win games. However, when players develop their skills and move up in age and skill level, our approach must be modified accordingly. Simple exercises that focus on technique alone can be perceived by elite players as monotonous as they are simply not challenged enough. Technique must always be practiced and perfected but if you can engage players as early in the training session as possible, your chances of keeping them absorbed in the process of practice will improve significantly.

Don't Miss The Point!

You always want energy and vigor from your players so let's look at creating that environment as soon as they walk onto the practice field. The goal of the warm-up should be to increase intensity levels towards high-tempo game specific movements with game intensity decision making and execution. We should be looking to propel our players into game mode as early as possible. We do this through a games focused warm-up that is designed to emphasize the key points that you will work on in your session.

There are a number of advantages to using a game focused approach in your warm-up:

1. There is a need for realism and constant transfer of game related training. Games enable players to experience situations that they encounter during actual match play. By experiencing these situations during practice, players can combine tactical, technical, physical, and mental aspects of their game early in the session. Players repeat the means of solving the problem rather than repeating the solution.

2. The games will allow you to evaluate prior understanding and ability levels. You can see what areas the players are proficient in, as well as breaking down individual or collective areas of concern.

3. Even though players enjoy games more, the physical demands can be tapered by the coach and can move towards high intensity loads if they choose to.

4. Players are programmed to 'switch on' for games. Arousal and anxiety levels typically increase and a competitive mindset will start to develop as they line up against one another. Again, these demands will be present at the start of every game.

5.   Increase in communication early in the session. Players will have to pass on information and encouragement to each other in game situations.

6.   In a game based warm-up, players will have to make more on-the-ball decisions than they would in a structured drill where the coach dictates every action. Controlled, open games are more cognitively demanding than closed drills.

Pre-Practice Dynamic Warm Up

Before our game based warm-up, our players should be physically and mentally prepared for practice. The objective of a warm-up should be to reduce the rate of injury but how can you go one step further and get your players ready with key physical components?

The majority of European clubs employ sports science and trainers to conduct a dynamic warm-up before the session begins. Players need to be physically ready for the training session, and almost every movement in soccer is preceded by an eccentric movement. It is very rare that the Head Coach will take this part of training as they are responsible for the main session.

Most young players prefer static stretching, but this does not optimize their time best. Recent research that measured the effects of static and dynamic stretching on sprinting ability during training showed that 15 minutes of dynamic stretching had no negative effects on sprint training. However, static stretching of the limbs and hip muscles resulted in a reduction in explosive power.

A dynamic warm-up is important and can be performed effectively as a routine. It prepares your body for performance by increasing flexion in the joints and increasing body temperature. A sports science specialist is not a necessity however. I have witnessed some great practice environments where the team captains take responsibility for the pre-practice warm-up, and I have taken this method and used it with my own teams. The biggest advantage of this type of warm-up is that it does not waste a minute of your actual training session!

Normally players arrive at practice about 20 minutes before it starts. They spend time socializing and waiting for you, the coach, to give them the starting signal. By the time your team begins practice with you, they can be distracted with all the social interaction and this causes concentration to be an issue. It can take time and a lot of energy for a coach to refocus a team. To prevent that dramatic loss in attentiveness before the session even begins, the solution is simple: have a structured dynamic warm-up that you can teach your team, and give responsibility to your team captain to conduct this before every session. You can always supervise from a distance to make sure everyone is doing what they need to be doing. By giving the players ownership, you are also making players accountable - so that they must look after their own bodies.

Sometimes players will look for a break in the session and request a stretch but this can be counterproductive and cause a decline in focus and tempo. Instead, the players must be aware that their pre-practice dynamic warm-up is important and vital for them to prepare for the session ahead.

Following a structured 15-20 minute dynamic stretch, your team should be ready physically and have gone through their mental routine to prepare for the session. Physically and mentally, they are ready for action. It is now up to you to add the technical and tactical elements as well as bringing the mental and physical ones up to game speed. Let's look at some game based warm-ups that will make sure your team hits the ground running!

Opposite Playing Styles Warm-Up: Possession v Pressure

This is a great game to warm-up with because it involves two contrasting styles of play and challenges the players to adapt and solve the problems associated with each.

Game Conditions:

Two teams play 5v5 in a 30x30 yard area with 5 yard channels. There are two outside channels with two target players in each. The possession-focused team (black shirts) are aiming to work the ball across the field from the target players on one outside channel to the other. They can also use the goalkeepers so this will create a 7v5 overload in the middle. Every time the possession-focused team works the ball across the field to the target players, they get 1 point. The counter attacking team (white shirts) are aiming to win the ball back as quickly as possible and upon doing so, can attack either goal.

Duration: Four games of three minutes. Teams change roles after every game.

Chapter 5

Coaching Points:

Team in Possession:

- Create angles to receive the ball
- Body shape to open up possession when possible
- Maintain a team shape/structure
- Transition when losing possession to prevent the opposition from scoring

Counter-Attacking Team:

- High pressure to win the ball back
- Defensive organization when pressing – don't get isolated
- Quick transition to create a shooting opportunity when the ball is won back.

Possession v Pressure Game

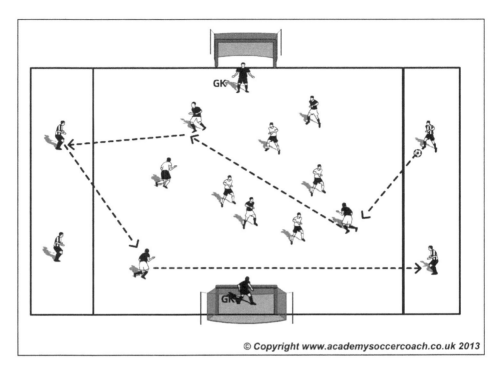

© Copyright www.academysoccercoach.co.uk 2013

As we can see in the diagram above, the team with black shirts - who are looking to work the ball across the field - must offer a number of options both wide and ahead of the ball. The player in possession should always receive the ball facing these options so he/she can play quickly and deal with the pressure from the team in white shirts.

Six Goal Transition Game

This multi-functional game tests speed of play, pressure, movement, decision making, and communication, as well as working together as a team. Every player has more than one defensive responsibility so must make sure they can see the situation develop and get to where they are needed quickly.

Game Conditions:

Two teams play 5v5 in the 30x20 yard middle area. The goalkeepers have a free zone where no other players are allowed to enter. Both goalkeepers are responsible for defending two goals each. The team in white shirts attacks the two bottom goals, and the team in black shirts attacks the two top goals. Both teams can score in the small goals in the outside.

Goalkeepers can move along the line to prevent goals and offer support to their team.

Duration: three games of four minutes with one minute recovery in-between.

Coaching Points:

- Defensive organization – each team needs to be in a position to stop each goal and not leave any player isolated. Although individual players can be responsible for one goal they also provide cover for teammates.

- Quick transitions – teams need to attack upon winning possession

- Decision Making – players need to solve problems quickly and get in positions both sides of the ball

- Offense – players need to look to change the point of attack through possession in the middle area

- Communication – individuals need to get organized quickly, especially the goalkeepers

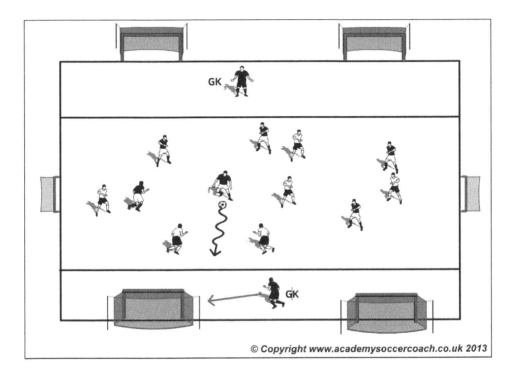

© Copyright www.academysoccercoach.co.uk 2013

Problem solving is a key element in this exercise. Players on both sides of the ball have to be aware of their roles and have a number of decisions to make. Keepers can help with those decisions by seeing the situations develop and by communicating to their teammates. The team that makes the quickest decisions will win.

Goalkeeper Quarterback Game

This game works on build-up play, movement off the ball, and has the goalkeepers making the 'killer pass'. Decision making is an important skill for keepers too, along with their distribution. Games like this challenge and work on those skills.

Game Conditions:

Teams play 9v9 on a full sized pitch (or smaller depending on age/quality of players). Goalkeepers are the only players allowed in the center circle and are restricted there.

In order to score, a team must first chip ball into their goalkeeper in the center circle, who must then start an attack by throwing or passing on the ground. No kicks out of hands allowed. Goalkeepers have four seconds before distributing. Both teams can score in any of the six goals.

Duration: play three games of five minutes with one minute recovery in-between.

Coaching Points:

- Pressure to stop the service into the goalkeeper
- Quality of the pass into keepers – the pass must be in the air
- Movement off the ball when keepers are in possession. Can you give them an option as quickly as possible?
- Change the point of attack through the goalkeeper
- Defensive work rate to prevent the opposing team from scoring

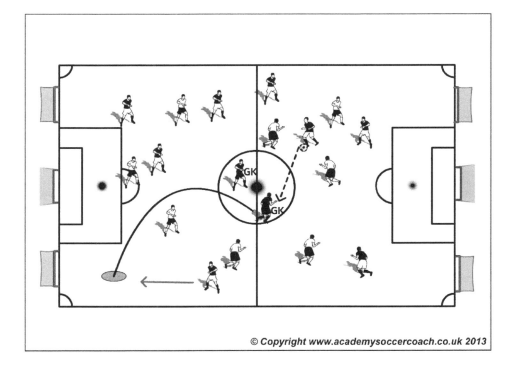

© Copyright www.academysoccercoach.co.uk 2013

Defensively, this is also a great game for concentration and decision making. Because both goalkeepers cannot move from the center circle, it is important that defensive pressure "shows" the players in possession away from the middle of the field. If they do break the pressure, the defensive team then needs to drop and cover the space in behind so they do not invite deep runs from attacking players.

Angles and Movement Game

This possession-based game focuses on decision making off the ball as much as it does on it. It challenges players to take up intelligent positions, and works on movement going forward. If the tempo of the game can be kept as high as possible, players will learn very quickly.

Game Conditions:

Teams play 7v7 on a 40x50 yard field. The field is coned into 10x10 squares both vertically and horizontally, so the whole playing area is a grid. The first condition is that players are not allowed to play the ball square to a team-mate in the same channel as them. With this condition, players will need to adjust their supporting angles.

The next condition is that players are not allowed to play in the same vertical or horizontal channel. This now means that players will have to work hard on and off the ball to make sure they are not in a poor position. The speed of the game will determine how hard they have to work so the higher the defensive pressure, the better.

No square passes and no straight runs. This game is all about intelligent movement along with quick decision making.

Duration: three games of four minutes with one minute recovery in-between.

Coaching Points:

- Decision making on the ball – scan the field early

- Supporting angles – take good positions that the player on the ball can find

- Communication – help each other out

- Goalkeeper – if they are to offer support, they must also move

- With these restrictions, can a player still attack at speed and with quality?

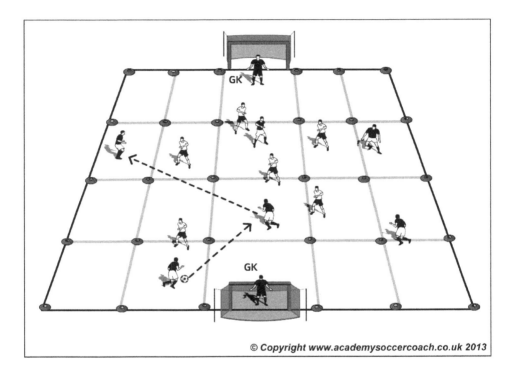

© Copyright www.academysoccercoach.co.uk 2013

Once players understand the movement and angles in the game, they should develop an understanding of space. As a result, players will have more time in possession and defenders will have to work a lot harder to close down areas. This should result in the creation of increased chances and goal scoring opportunities.

Early Cross Game

If players know there is service coming in early, it puts the focus on them to get into attacking positions in the penalty box as soon as possible. Too often our wide players are forced to chase passes aimed towards the corner flag and, after gaining possession of the ball, barely have enough energy to produce a cross. This game focuses on the service to wide players' feet - ahead of the service.

Game Conditions:

Teams play 7v7 in a 50x70 area. Both teams will have two wide attacking players in a 5x5 yard box in the wide attacking area of the field. In order for both teams to score, they must first play the ball into either box in which their team has a player. The players inside the box are limited to two touches – one to control and one to cross. Goals must come from a cross.

Goalkeepers cannot play straight into the boxes. There must first be a build-up involving the outfield players. Players inside the box cannot leave.

Duration: three games of four minutes with one minute recovery in-between.

Coaching Points:

- Quality of passing to the players inside the box

- Quality and type of cross. If crosses are coming in early, there should be space between defense and keeper. Is it necessary that the cross is lofted in the air?

- Defensive pressure. Can the defending team 'show' the player in possession away from threatening areas?

- Movement. As crosses are coming in quickly, players have to get into attacking options as swiftly as possible

- Transition. With crosses coming in quickly, the goalkeeper will have a huge role in starting the next attack. It is vital that the keepers' speed of play matches the intensity of the players.

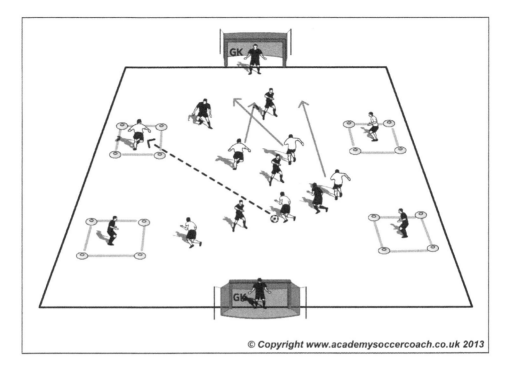

As soon as the ball is played to an attacking player inside the 5x5 box, encourage as many players as possible to get into the penalty area as quickly as possible. This will result in overloads in attacking areas and increased chances of goals. It is an attacking game so the team that commits the most numbers forward will have a good chance of success.

Summary

Inter Milan and Argentine veteran, Javier Zanetti, told FourFourTwo magazine when comparing the differences in training that he has experienced in his distinguished career; "Twenty years ago every training session began with a four or five-mile run. Now everything involves the ball. Science is more advanced, and allows us to train and play at my peak."

It is no coincidence that the best players in the world are exposed to the best training programs. As coaches, we are all borderline obsessive about details and how to give our team an edge or a competitive advantage when it comes to the game. There is no better way to do that than by teaching our players how to prepare for performance, both mentally and physically. If you want your players to consistently start games on the front foot, with vigor and energy, then they have to start your training sessions in the same manner. The motivational message before kick-off can still work, in moderation, but that method of encouragement should accompany detailed routines that your players are aware of and which can prepare their bodies for performance.

Once players are physically prepared for action, complementing this with technical, tactical, and mental focus should now be the goal. And don't forget about the tempo – there are physical differences between a warm-up and high intensity work, so you also have to create an environment where players can move to the next level physically too. This is why game based warm-ups are so beneficial.

The buck stops with the coach. How the team develops preparation habits is down to your training program. If the session is not planned well and the coach does not state objectives, game based warm-ups can even lead to reduced individual skill practice volume. You have to maximize your every minute on the practice field and approach it in the same manner as you do the 89th minute on a game day. That urgency, passion, and enthusiasm for the game should always be expressed in how you work with your team throughout the week. It's infectious!

Once you get your team approaching and preparing for sessions in the right way, games become easier and performances become more consistent. When you come out of your games based warm-up, the players are right where you want them. They are ready to keep that intensity going, open to your ideas, and prepared to lift the level even higher to see what you have prepared for them next. Let's make sure we don't disappoint them!

6

Scoring Goals

Goals change games. No doubt about it. Scoring them has been, and always will be, the toughest thing to do in a soccer game. That is why people who can do it on the biggest stage are rewarded with lucrative contracts, endorsements and celebrity status. As coaches, we always appreciate players who can put the ball in the net when it really matters but do we effectively look at how we can develop players who can do it? This is an important question because we will more than likely not be fortunate enough to have a world-class forward or a 'natural goal scorer' on our team, so learning to create chances has got to be a part of our training plan.

Like any other talent in sport, scoring goals is a matter of repetition, routine, and making sure the player with the job of scoring has composure and a cool head to take the opportunity presented. When I study the greatest goalscorers, both past and present, I put their success down to three elements:

1. Technique

2. Temperament

3. Service

None of the qualities above are innate and each one can be developed with effective, deliberate practice. It does not matter if you are Van Basten, Romario, Ronaldo, Abby Wambach, or Mia Hamm, scoring goals is more of a science than an art. Now granted, the players above were blessed with extraordinary physical gifts and talent to perform at the highest stage, but that does not mean that they did not spend hours upon hours honing their craft in front of goal.

Chapter 6

Four Dimensions Of Attacking Soccer

Scoring goals is about habits and modern coaching techniques can develop those habits effectively and efficiently. In order for your team to create chances and score goals, your attacking work on the practice field must stay consistent with the four dimensional approach of modern coaching. Every attacking session should therefore include the following components:

Technical

There is always a high quality, technical component involved in the majority of goals scored in elite games. If the quality is not actually the finish itself, it is almost certainly from either a cross from a wide area, a through ball from midfield, or a passing interchange with another teammate. In the same way, poor technique has waved many a good opportunity goodbye, for example a shot blazing over the bar from a short distance out or a rushed cross that does not clear the first defender. You therefore have to make sure that when players get into good attacking areas, they can execute the skill despite limited time and space. If the technical areas are addressed at the right times during practice, you will see a vast improvement in games. With elite players, you do not need to stop the session when a forward leans back when shooting causing the ball to rise over the bar, but the reminders need to be there all the time. If the problem persists, work with the individual after the session and try not to disrupt attacking sessions with frequent stoppages.

Tactical

Tactical and physical aspects are very closely related when working on attacking soccer with your team. No matter what formation you play, every tactical system has a way of scoring goals and creating chances. Not every training session, however, shows the players exactly how effective that system can be when everyone is working together. You have to teach this, but in an effective manner conducive to the demands of the modern game. For example, if we walk through a number of tactical scenarios with our team, it can help players understand, but it does not replicate the speed of the game. By adding game like tempo however, we can challenge players to see the tactical pictures a lot quicker and this might buy them that extra split second on the ball that can prove to be the difference. Also, tactical work causes attacking players to develop mental triggers which can allow them to recognize scenarios as they develop in games and be very difficult to defend against. Other tactical aspects that need to be considered in order to score goals are how the team is going to create chances. Once an attacking player knows where chances will be created within the framework of the system, he/she will find goalscoring chances more plentiful and will not be surprised when they arrive.

Physical

When playing at a high level, space in the attacking third is like gold dust, especially in today's game where the top teams can get numbers organized behind the ball very quickly. The one solution against rigid, organized defenses is movement: involving both the ball and the players. The more movement from an attacking team, the more problems presented to defenders. Movement creates space, which usually causes chances to be created. However, if players are going to constantly move ahead of the ball and get into dangerous positions, they need to have the physical capabilities to do so. When working on attacking soccer, there should always be a physical challenge for your players. They have to get ahead of the ball, get into the final third as quickly as possible, change direction, and they have to be willing to make a number of those runs and *not* get the ball every time. As a center forward, Alan Shearer believed that he had to make 13 forward runs to receive the ball once. That is an incredible commitment to the physical side of the game. Although it is hard work, the good news is that everyone loves going forward so all players want to get involved!

Mental

The most important goals happen when the player who scores keeps a level head amid all the chaos going on around him/her. Remember Ryan Giggs' famous goal celebration against Arsenal in 1999, running half the length of the field with his shirt off with so much emotion and adrenaline that no one could catch him? That kind of raw emotion was nowhere to be seen just thirty seconds before as he danced through seven Arsenal players before rifling a left foot shot, cold as ice, past goalkeeper David Seaman. The lesson here is that top attacking players respond to emotion by focusing on technique. And if your players are going to score a last minute goal with huge stakes on the line, you need them to do the same. The mental piece of scoring goals is vital. Like a golfer, too much emotion will cause their execution to go wayward. Instead, if your attacking players can focus on technique when it is most needed, they will be rewarded with goals. Another hugely important mental aspect directly related to scoring goals is confidence. Every time a top class forward goes through a barren spell in front of goal, everyone talks about a drop in confidence as the reason. Although it will help forwards score goals, confidence will not show up and knock on your door. It comes as a result of being prepared to take your chances, which comes from quality work on the practice field and is transferred into games. The best players create their own confidence, and they know where to find it if it goes missing.

The Standards You Set

Winning teams come to practice with a process goal. The best coaches communicate and get the players to buy into that process every time they step onto the field. No player ever got better at scoring goals by doing it less, therefore our practices have to consistently work on effective ways to score and create chances.

Pleasure Always Has To Outweigh the Pressure

All players love scoring goals, but too many are scared to fail because of the burden placed on them by coaches or outside pressure. Your attacking sessions have to inspire creativity and enjoyment in your players so that they are having so much fun, they do not have enough time to worry about the outcome. It is very easy to achieve this when your session is multi-functional and involves more than one technical, physical action or decision for the player to perform. Also, when there is a competitive element to the attacking session, it can help players focus on what their team needs to win the game. Above all, your reaction to goals scored can be critical. Be enthusiastic and positive when good attacking play occurs in practice or in games. Again remember, what gets recognized gets repeated.

Find Your Danger Zone

This is something for you to look at specifically with your group of players and your preferred system of play. Where can your team be most effective going forward? How do you foresee your team scoring goals? Are your players getting into dangerous areas inside the penalty area or are they going in there to simply make the numbers up? Your answers to these questions will establish the attacking standards and expectations that you have for your team and whether or not you will be successful in creating chances and ultimately taking advantage of them.

If you have not identified specific danger areas for your players to take up, they will struggle to find them. Teams typically score in one of three ways; from wide areas (Manchester United under Sir Alex Ferguson), from intricate passing inside the perimeters of the 18 yard box (Arsenal/Barcelona), or long passes over the top of a defense (Liverpool with Gerrard and Torres). When you establish how your team can create the most opportunities, it is important that the players know roles and responsibilities going forward.

The Importance of Tap-In Goals!

If scoring goals is high on your list of priorities with your team, you have to stress the importance of opportunities within the six yard box. Goals at the top level are hard enough to come by but we all know that they count the same regardless of whether they are scored from 30 yards or 3 yards.

One of the reasons why we have very few "natural" goalscorers in the game today, I believe, is because the majority of practice sessions overlook the importance of scoring "ugly" goals. Too often we work on attacking play and when the move is interrupted or not finished in the perfect way, we disregard that phase of play and look towards the next attack in the hope of executing perfection. The problem with this is twofold: 1) Fewer players are willing to 'gamble' and follow up attacks to the penalty box. 2) When chances do arise, players in the right positions are taken by surprise because they never find themselves in similar positions on the practice field.

Three years ago, I made a conscious decision to focus on goals from rebounds, goalmouth scrambles, and simply opportunistic runs when the ball looked like being delivered into the area. Not only did I see an increase in goals, but they proved to be vital goals that brought our team important league wins in difficult games. If the ball is going to bounce inside that six yard box, I want one of my players to react first! Again, this is truly a habit.

Chapter 6

Be Careful To Criticize!

When working with your team on attacking and forward play, balance is the key. You want your players to focus and concentrate on technique and getting in position, but you also do not want pressure weighing down the players and their attempts on goal. No burden is heavier to carry in soccer than that of a forward who has not scored in a long time. The practice field has to be where they can rehearse success, and not failure, going into the game. How you talk to them, coach them, and react to their mistakes or goals can be crucial to the mental game. An essential part of creativity is not being afraid to fail. Former Manchester United manager, Sir Alex Ferguson, refused to criticize a player in the final third during training sessions because negativity stifles creativity. Part of coaching is releasing energy and freedom. Keep it positive and if your players fail to score in the game, they can enjoy practicing and visualizing success on the practice field with you.

Attacking Exercise 1

This exercise works on a number of aspects needed to score goals. There is the build-up play, getting numbers in dangerous areas, the timing of runs into the middle, and the quality of the cross and finish.

Set-Up:

The play takes place on one half of the field, involving four players at a time. This allows you to put the players into specific areas that you feel they will be effective, or gives you the option to rotate.

Forwards work in pairs (A and B) and begin the exercise as Player B plays a long pass to Player C. As soon as the pass is played, Players A and B, begin to sprint to the poles ahead of them. At the same time, Player C controls and passes to Player D.

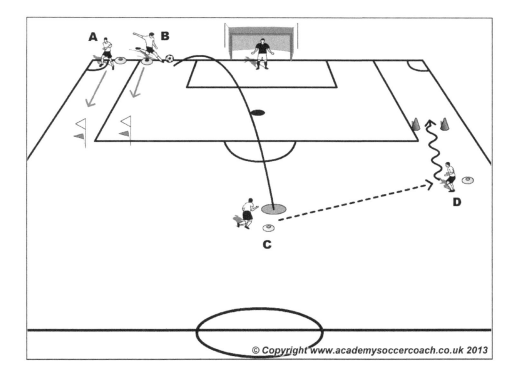

Chapter 6

As soon as Player D receives the ball, he/she must drill towards the gate ahead at full speed. Simultaneously, Players A and B run around the poles and now head into the penalty box (Player B attacking the near post and Player A attacking the far post). Player C also joins in the attack coming in late towards the penalty box to pick up any delivery that is behind the forwards. There should be a quick cross once Player D comes out of the gates and Players A, B, and C should finish on goal.

Coaching Points:

- Everything done at full speed.
- The earlier the cross comes in, the more physical work Players A, B and C have to do. Challenge them to attack those areas!
- Relaxed finish – if the pace is on the cross, no need to meet it with power.

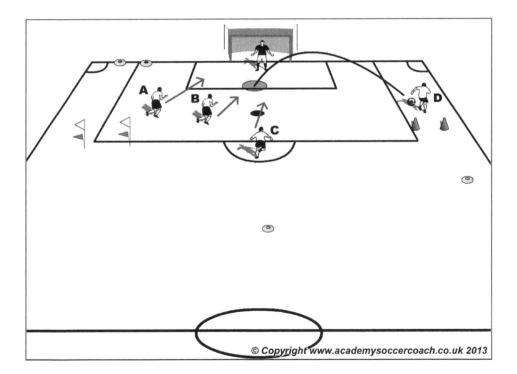

Attacking Exercise 2

This exercise also challenges players to multi-task on the field. There is a skill element, physical element, and a test of focus and concentration to execute each skill effectively.

Set-Up:

The exercise takes place in one half of the field, using two goals, two goalkeepers, and a good supply of balls. Players are put into two lines (see the positions of Player A and Player B). On the coach's signal, both Players A and B start at the same time; Player A dribbles up to the mannequin, performs a move, and then shoots on goal. Player B must dribble through the cones and drive through the gate ahead.

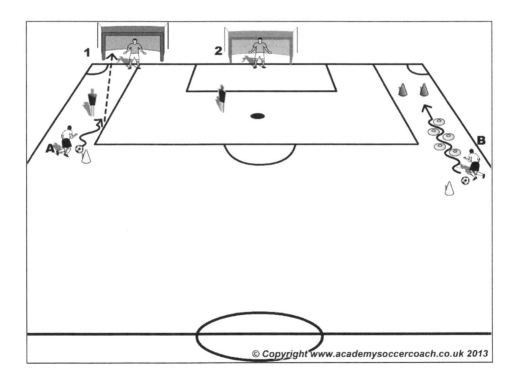

© Copyright www.academysoccercoach.co.uk 2013

Chapter 6

Following the shot, Player A must get across the mannequin and attack the near post. At the same time, Player B will be coming out of the gates and must now deliver a cross for Player A to finish on goal. After the second ball is finished, the next group begins.

Coaching Points:

- The faster players challenge themselves; faster is tougher to execute technically - so push the tempo all the time.
- The cross must be played in with pace towards the near post. Any cross lofted high or 'underhit' will be collected by the goalkeeper.
- Player A must time his/her run across the near post. Don't get in too early!

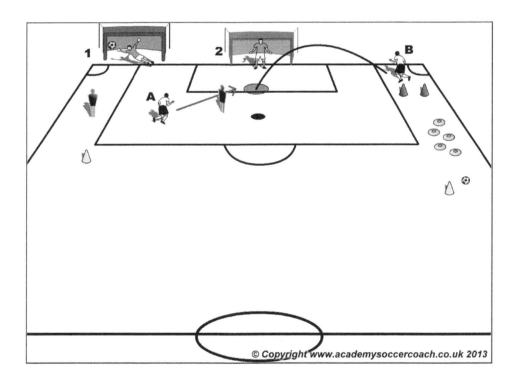

Attacking Exercise 3

When you play against top level competition, long diagonal balls towards your wide attacking players will rarely break down a defensive back four. Multiple player movement, however, will always cause defending teams problems. This exercise challenges players to build up the play at speed, and offer support angles ahead of the ball.

Set-Up:

The exercise takes place in one half of the field. Players are divided into three groups. Player A starts by passing to Player B and then sprinting towards Player C. Player B opens up quickly and passes to Player C.

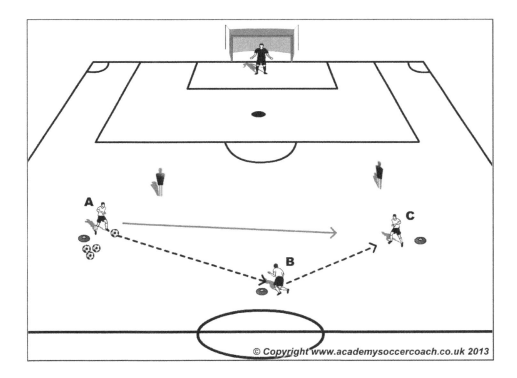

© Copyright www.academysoccercoach.co.uk 2013

Chapter 6

As soon as Player B passes, he/she must sprint around the far mannequin and get into the box. When the ball arrives at Player C, so too does Player A. They play a short give and go, and Player A sets Player C into a wide area. Player A must now get into the box quickly. Player C gets the cross in as soon as possible towards the penalty spot, where Players A and B should be arriving to finish.

Coaching Points:

- Everything is done at full speed to put pressure on the cross to come in early and to challenge Players A and B to get into the box early.
- The quality of passes and crossing must be high. Speed of play is important but quality of play is vital!

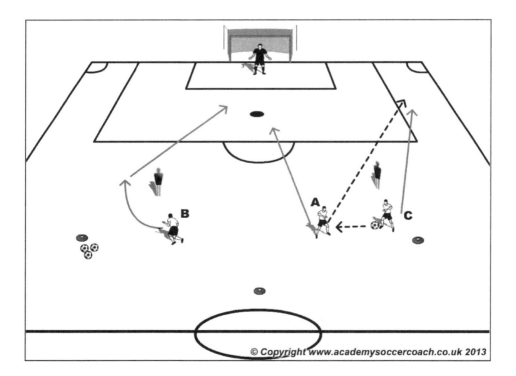

© Copyright www.academysoccercoach.co.uk 2013

Attacking Exercise 4

This exercise takes care of most aspects of goalscoring. There are three parts: the "killer pass" through a defense, a cross from a wide area, and a shot from long distance. As with all four dimensional exercises, none of these skills are practiced in isolation and the players must all work together and react quickly.

Set-Up:

The exercise takes place in one half of the field and works four players at a time (Players A,B,C and D). Three players serve, two from a wide area and one from the goal line. The exercise starts with a short combination play between Players A, B, and C, which allows Player C to play the "killer pass" to Player D who times his run from deep and finishes on goal.

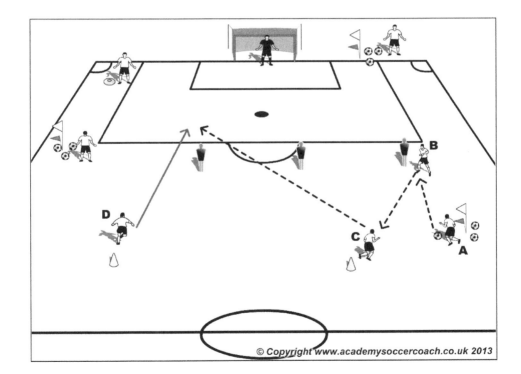

© Copyright www.academysoccercoach.co.uk 2013

Chapter 6

As soon as Player D finishes on goal, Players A and B must sprint into the box. The second wave of attack then begins quickly as the two players out wide combine for a cross. As soon as the second attack ends, Player D has timed his run to the edge of the penalty box and now receives a ball from the goal line server to strike first time.

Coaching Points:

- Game Speed! Quick combination play and quick transition between all three types of service.
- Execution of each finish. Focus on technique at the right time and do not rush it!
- Set your team the target of three goals in a row. Tough challenge!

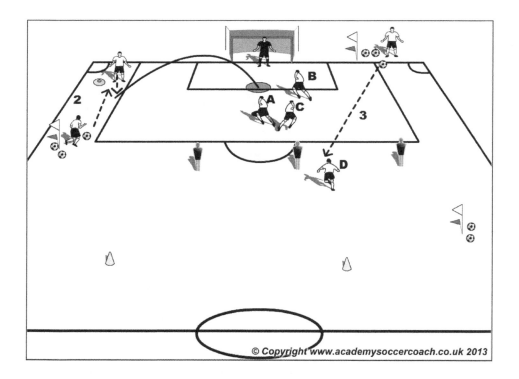

© Copyright www.academysoccercoach.co.uk 2013

Attacking Exercise 5

This multi-function exercise is complex but involves all the skills needed to attack effectively within the final third. Each player has two responsibilities throughout the exercise so it challenges them to think quickly and focus.

Set-Up:

The exercise takes place in one half of the field. There are three groups of players at A, B, and C, with a server out wide and a goalkeeper. On the coach's signal, player A must drive towards the mannequin, perform a trick, and then shoot on goal. After the shot, Player A must sprint around towards the server and Player B plays a lofted pass to Player C. Player C controls it and shoots on goal from a wider angle.

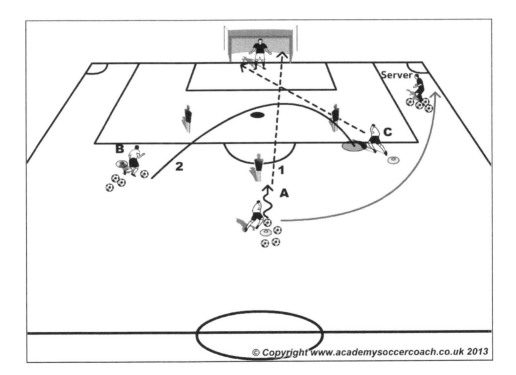

© Copyright www.academysoccercoach.co.uk 2013

Chapter 6

Following the second shot, Player C must sprint towards the far post and player B must sprint towards the near post. Player A has now arrived at the server and crosses a ball first time for Players B and C to finish the third attempt on goal. Players return to the same line and rotate after four minutes.

Coaching Points:

- Focus and Concentration – If one player switches off, the exercise breaks down.
- Don't let the speed of the exercise take away from the quality. Go as fast as you can but do not rush the execution.
- Player A's cross must be across the six yard box, no need to look up. Deliver early!

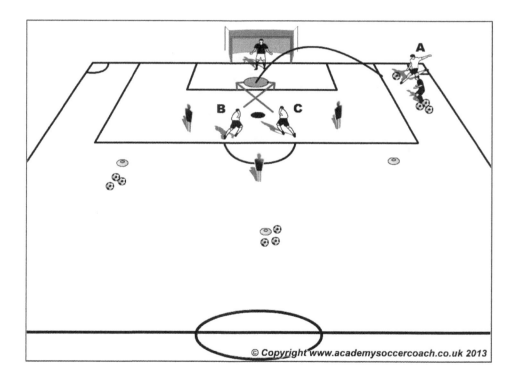

Summary

Sometimes the smallest margins bring the greatest and most memorable moments in the game. That's why it is worth working so hard and doing it right. If your sessions are centered on possession exercises with no opportunities to shoot or finish in front of goal, you are giving up these margins and starving your forwards of the opportunity to create successful habits in front of goal.

We cannot afford to put our players through monotonous shooting exercises where they simply hit one shot and go to the back of a long line. Instead, you must challenge your players to perform more than one task in every attacking exercise that you do with your team. The more your exercises demand high quality movement, concentration, and build-up play, the better your players will be in front of goal.

Goal scoring is a by-product of doing the right things every day on the practice field. It all comes down to routines: the movement which can create a crucial yard, the exact areas where we expect the right type of service, and that focus on technique at the decisive moment. With multi-functional exercises you also work on attacking in different ways which will benefit your players as they can adjust to the demands of the game.

Attacking exercises should be fun for players and coaches alike. If you are positive and creative with your session ideas, your players will produce the same in games. You must still drive the session with high standards, but most of the demands are in the exercises themselves. Nothing drives attacking teams more than confidence. Once your team starts scoring goals and associating it with your training, your team will go to a whole new level. Then all you need to worry about is stopping them at the other end!

7
Defending

Remember when defending used to be simply about stopping the other team from scoring? If the names Stiles, Rattin, Gentile, Goikoetxea, or Butcher sound familiar, you grew up in an era where the physical approach of defending trended during every World Cup tournament from the 1960s right through to the 1990s. We turned on the TV to watch the greatest players in the world but it felt like these guys were there solely to stop them from playing. And maybe they were. The rules were stretched to the extreme and the onus was very much on man marking and being destructive. Thankfully for supporters of attacking soccer, defending changed significantly when two FIFA laws were introduced. By altering off-side rules, defenders could no longer rely on simply pushing up and raising their hands to relieve the pressure on their teams. There was also a clampdown on robust defending as attacking players received more protection from referees. Today's game has almost developed into a non-contact sport and players, as well as coaches, have had to adapt to defending in the modern era.

The principles of team defending have also changed in recent years. You no longer see teams relying on a simple central defender pairing to keep out opponents. In order for a team to keep a clean sheet/ shutout, teams are now required to defend together. This can be done in a number of ways: pressing high, absorbing pressure, counter attacking, and even countering the counter attack. Whatever the system, it is imperative that all eleven players fulfill their roles. Barcelona, Chelsea, and most recently both German giants Bayern Munich and Borussia Dortmund have revolutionized how we approach the defensive side of the game. Along with the technological advances at almost every level, teams who have weaknesses in any part of the field will most likely get exposed week-in and week-out as TV analysts cannot wait to pinpoint defensive frailties. There is now little room for error when defending.

Four Dimensions of Defending

Before you plan your defensive exercises, you must first look at how your own defenders will be challenged during games. This may change due to playing level, opponents' playing style, or your own team's playing style, but in many ways the fundamental demands will always be very similar. At youth level, defenders usually excel in the physical side of the game. When you get to elite and professional levels however, the best defenders are proficient in technique, possession, decision making, and concentration because the modern game demands it. Working solely on one dimension of defending without a link or progression to the big picture will not develop individuals or teams. Yes, some defenders will need work in certain areas, but keep the four dimensional approach present in the majority of your sessions and you will see vast improvements in games.

Technical

The speed of the modern game punishes defensive mistakes quickly, and without mercy, at the highest level. Defenders today need almost faultless technique – good 1v1 defending, effective reading of the game, capable of dealing with overloads, and patience to name but a few. Balance is also important as defenders have to restrict the space of attacking players, but at the same time they have to be careful of getting too tight because forwards can spin off, turn, and are very difficult to catch if they get away. Maybe the biggest technical point of modern defending is how to stop players without 'leaving your feet' and committing yourself to the tackle. If you go to ground with a slide tackle in today's game, you run the risk of free kicks, penalties and yellow cards. In possession, the demands on modern defenders are higher than ever. Opta's figures show that defenders averaged 63 touches of the ball per 90 minutes in the 2010–11 Premier League season, with midfielders on 73 and forwards down to 51. This means that defenders are finding themselves in possession more and more, so distribution must be of high quality. Strength in the air is still an important skill and the ability to be brave and block shots is an asset that goalkeepers and coaches appreciate from any member of their back four.

Tactical

Systems of play and formations today demand that all players defend together as one unit, rather than simply leaving it to your back four to do all the "dirty work". In order to win in modern soccer, you need eleven players committed to the defensive side of the game. You can no longer have passengers on your team; players who are unwilling to work for the cause have found themselves as disposable assets regardless of their attacking qualities. Every player must know what is expected of them and the team. You only have to look at Luis Suarez and Carlos Tevez's work rate to see how attackers have become the first line of defense. The other tactical advances in the game today are the concepts of pressure and counter attacking defending. Defending has become more complex as teams now look at the space between their back four and their furthest attacking player to become as compact as possible. This makes playing against such teams very difficult. Without a tactical understanding of defending, a team will be exposed when the opposition changes their attacking system. When Manchester United went down to ten men against Real Madrid during their Champions League clash in March 2013, they failed to adapt defensively to combat Madrid's extra man in midfield. As a result, Luca Modric became a focal point with more time on the ball and, fifteen minutes and two Madrid goals later, the game was over.

Physical

To stop teams from scoring in the modern game, the physical demands on both the team and individual players has increased enormously. Can you imagine the fitness levels needed to pressure teams as relentlessly as Barcelona does for 90 minutes? It takes an enormous amount of energy, stamina, and aerobic capacity to do this effectively. The concept of speed has changed with regards to defending in the modern game. Coaches used to be concerned with having players who were quick enough to recover and deal with the space behind the back four. However, today coaches focus more on the space in front of the back four as a time and space has become such an important commodity. As the physical demands on players and teams have evolved, so too must the type of physical training required to defend effectively in the modern game. Physical training needs to focus on covering shorter distances and changing direction multiple times at maximum speed with minimal time for recovery.

Mental

The mental and physical components go hand in hand when discussing defending in the modern game. A mental error can be just as costly as a physical one and as fatigue sets in towards the end of the game, mental mistakes are never far away. If one player does not fulfill his/her defensive responsibility, space can open up and this can prove costly. Defenders are also asked to multi-task in today's game, both offensively and defensively. This means they have to take on more information, use the ball well, constantly be aware of shape in and out of possession, and communicate with their defensive partners on who is picking up whom, among a host of other responsibilities. Opportunities to rest for defenders are few and far between, because as soon as they win a corner or a set-piece, they usually have to travel to the opposition penalty area and fulfill an attacking role. With so many demands during the game, concentration has become an essential asset for a top-class defender. Although it is virtually impossible to maintain full concentration for 90 plus minutes, defenders must be able to focus for short amounts of time, break, and refocus again as quickly as possible. If your training environment can reflect the same challenges that a game will bring, your defenders will be conditioned to focus and refocus at the right time, hence reducing the likelihood of concentration lapses happening on gameday.

The Standards You Set

Without demanding certain high standards on the practice field, you cannot expect your team to be solid defensively week-in week-out. The difference between these standards and simple coaching points will be measured in the inconsistency of your team's defending. Stick with the standards below and a defensive mindset will be created and sustained in your team.

What is Effective Pressure?

Experienced players know the difference between good and bad execution of the skills required in a game. An off-balance shot, a poorly completed pass, a misjudged header, are all universally known by players as they are reinforced from an early age. However, by comparison, the definition of effective pressure is rarely discussed between players and coaches. We do not explain to our players the difference between pressuring, delaying, and simply standing back and allowing our opponent to do as they please. This leads to a discrepancy between what the coach wants and what the defensive player actually does.

There are three types of pressure that you must distinguish between, for your players. Once you establish the differences, you must explain where, and when, you want the right type of pressure in the game itself. Discuss matters with your players, practice them in game specific exercises with good feedback, and then set high demands every time you work with your team.

High Pressure: This is when the defensive player gets within a yard of the attacking player and aggressively looks to win the ball back or force the player into a mistake. The player in possession of the ball now has to put his/her head down to focus on the ball and cannot see the field or any supporting players. The defending player can apply physical pressure and should be in a position to win the ball within 3-5 seconds. This is real pressure!

Medium Pressure: This is when the defensive player is between 3-5 yards of the attacking player. The goal for the defender is to channel the player in possession into another area of the field. Holding midfielders do this a lot and this type of defending also occurs in wide areas of the field as full-backs wait for defensive support before they commit themselves to high pressure. It is certainly more effective higher up the field where players with a couple of yards of space cannot hurt you as much. Delay defending will be punished by attacking teams if it is attempted in the final third.

Low Pressure: This is when the defensive player is over 5 yards away from the player in possession. The defending player may be blocking space but is allowing the attacking player the time and space to play long or short, and to the right or left side. This is a dangerous way to defend because you do not restrict the attacking player's options except the path straight ahead. Goals can happen from anywhere on the field if your players are conditioned to defend like this.

Reorganize Quickly!

The traditional defensive practice exercise (see below) where we put our back four and goalkeeper to defend against a superior number of forwards and ask them to try and keep them at bay has its limits when it comes to effectiveness in the modern game. Yes, it can work on establishing roles and responsibilities, moving as a unit, and communicating successfully, but after these points are recognized with your team, you must progress the exercise because the game demands it.

Ideally, the progression will include an overload in attacking numbers and/or challenging our defense to get organized quickly, delaying before help arrives, and recovering as fast as possible. The reason for this is that counter attacks and transitions (which we will cover in detail in Chapters 8 and 9) are at the very heart of the modern game. As your team progresses, you may play against systems of play that will lure you in and try to get you to commit numbers forward, so they can plan on hitting you on the break. If your team is slow to reorganize, there will be spaces that top-class opposition will be able to exploit. In order to help your team reorganize quickly, you will need to highlight the importance of recovery runs and how to get numbers back behind the ball as soon as you lose possession. Coaching your team how to defend 'out of balance' will challenge them to solve problems quickly and effectively.

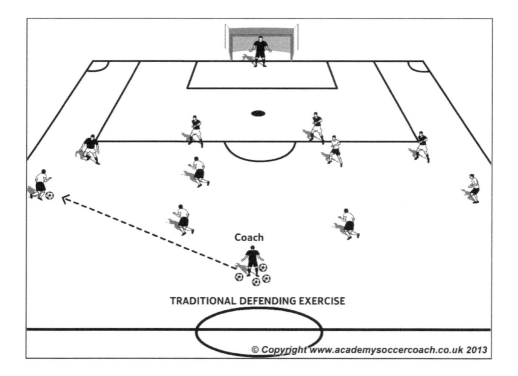

TRADITIONAL DEFENDING EXERCISE

Final Product of Defending

Another criticism of the traditional 'attack versus defense' exercise (above) is the fact that the defending team deals with the same type of attack time after time. After defenders take care of the first ball, there is a break before the exercise is restarted with the coach – usually when everyone is ready to go. The problem with this is that this scenario is not consistent with the game itself because, in the exercise, players never have to alter their recovery position to deal with the next attack. Instead, they go back to where they started which takes no focus or mental energy. The exercise therefore conditions the players to "switch off" and drop their levels of concentration after each attack as they subconsciously know where they will go when the attack is over.

You have to develop performance routines where your players understand that, like attacking, there is also a final product to defending. Defenders can opt to go long and direct to relieve the pressure on their team, or they can try to pass and play their way out. With both options however, there must be a tactical reaction made by the whole defensive unit. If they are looking to pass out of trouble, the team must move and give angles to support the player in possession. Alternatively, if the defender decides to go long to get rid of the pressure, the team must step up and shift in accordance to how far the ball travelled. Therefore, your exercises must have a way for defenders to condition themselves to keep playing after the clearance and, either be prepared for the second wave of attack, or transition into offense and help their team attack at the other end.

Ultimately the way you are training your defense may be counterproductive in the long term, particularly if they are developing bad habits. As Terry Venables once famously said, "practice makes permanent" so you must look for realism and quality in your defensive coaching. You have to challenge your players to make decisions, transition, and refocus as quickly as possible and in relation to where the next attack is coming from. Sessions that test players physically and technically may not test tactical and mental components if they can simply wander back to the starting point and await the coach's signal. Defenders must learn that there are a variety of attacks that they will need to defend and they cannot be certain when those tests will come.

Defensive Exercise 1

This is a great exercise to establish what effective pressure is, to develop a high work rate without the ball, and to work defensively in small groups. It is physically demanding and players must solve the problems as quickly as possible or else the workload increases dramatically. As a coach, it allows you to see what players can withstand pressure to a high standard because those that cannot will be exposed in an exercise like this.

Set-Up:

The team is split into three teams of six. Teams 1 and 3 occupy a 20x30 area and Team 2 is split with three players at one gate (Team 2A) in the middle and the other three players (Team 2B) at the other gate. The coach will serve and can start on either side.

Team 2 is working defensively first. Team 2A will always pressure the team to their right (Team 1) and Team 2B will also always pressure to their right (Team 3).

The coach will serve five balls each alternatively to Team 1 and Team 3. When Team 2A are working, Team 2B are recovering at the gate and vice versa.

Goals:

The defending teams (2A and 2B) must win the ball back as soon as possible. When each defensive team wins five balls they have completed the defensive part of the exercise and can rotate out. That is the goal for the defensive team.

However, if the team in possession makes more than six consecutive passes, the coach will add another ball to their total, thus keeping the defending team in for longer.

After both teams win the required number of balls back, rotate with Team 1 or Team 3. The coach can add a competition element to the exercise by timing how long each team is in the defensive part of the exercise. The team which is in the defensive part for the shortest period - wins.

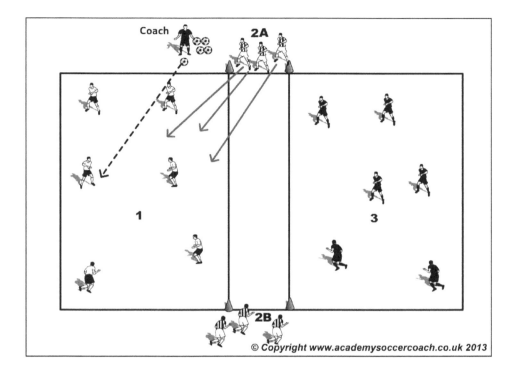

© Copyright www.academysoccercoach.co.uk 2013

Coaching Points:

- The quicker the pressure - the better; so get there early!

- Work as teams defensively! If one player is disconnected, the remaining two players will find it difficult to win the ball back.

- No passive pressure! You must win the ball at some stage.

- Communicate defensively with one another at all times.

- Always jog back to the gate to recover, to establish good habits.

Defensive Exercise 2

Coaches always talk about the importance of possession and how taxing it is physically when you do not have the ball. This exercise illustrates this perfectly. If you continue to give away possession here, your workload will be multiplied, in a similar fashion to Exercise 1.

Set-Up:

Three 10x10 grids are set up in a triangle formation. Six players partner up in groups and label themselves teams A, B, and C. The exercise starts with a 4v2, teams A and B against team C (in pinnies/bibs). All three groups start at the same time. When the defensive pair win the ball, the player that gave possession away must go along with their partner to the next grid and become the defender.

The three groups wait until all defending teams win the ball in every grid and then the players who conceded possession must move from grid 1 to 2, 2 to 3, 3 to 1.

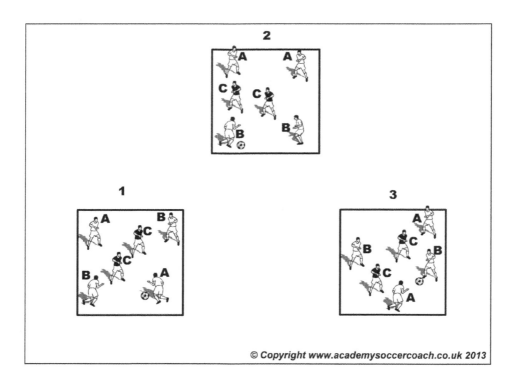

Coaching Points:

- The quicker the defensive team win the ball, the more time they will have to rest so there should be a sense of urgency in winning the ball back.

- There is now a responsibility between teammates to keep possession. This pressure should keep groups alert and should help raise the tempo.

- When the defending pair work together, they should never 'get split' with one pass through the middle of them both. Instead, when one player presses, the other should drop at an angle to take away the 'splitting' pass. This will reduce the options of the player in possession.

- Encourage communication at all times. Defenders should be identifying who is applying pressure on the ball and which player should drop. Good habits are created here!

Progressions:

- Have a forfeit for the defensive team if they cannot win the ball back within 20 seconds. Again, the more urgency you add to the exercise, the more game realistic it becomes and more players will condition themselves to work at a high intensity.

- Making the grids bigger will also make the defensive work more difficult and physically demanding.

Defensive Exercise 3

The ideal progression for the defending team, after they apply high pressure to win the ball, must then be to find a teammate and transition into attack. If the high-pressure defensive exercises continue to allow defenders to simply win by kicking the ball out of the grids, they will consequently struggle in the conversion from attack to defense during games. This exercise rewards defenders who can win the ball back quickly and complete a pass to a teammate in space, just like the game itself demands.

Set-Up:

Players are split into two teams of eight inside a 40x20 yard grid just outside the 18 yard box. There is also a goalkeeper positioned in the goal. The exercise is organized with eight black shirts against four white shirts inside the grid. The remaining four players on the white team take a position in the corners between the cones, and are labeled A, B, C and D below.

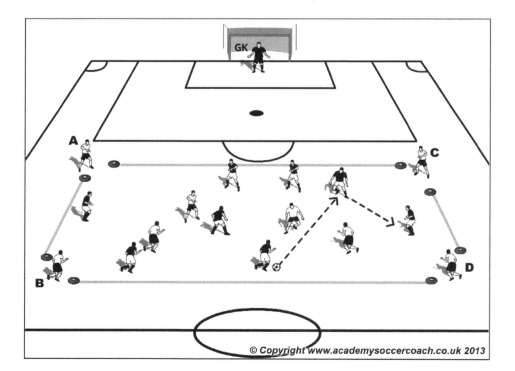

The goal for the eight players in black shirts is to complete six consecutive passes inside the grid, before breaking out of the grid and finishing on goal. No defensive player can leave the grid to chase an attacker headed towards goal.

The goal for the defending team in white shirts is to win back five completed balls. In order for them to be completed, they must win the ball and pass it to an outside teammate (A, B, C, or D) in the corner. If the attacking team scores however, this adds an extra ball to the exercise and therefore keeps the defending team inside the grid for a longer period.

After the defending team wins five completed balls back to the outside players, they rotate with the outside players. After they finish, the groups then switch roles.

Coaching Points:

-   The exercise rewards defensive pressure that can win the ball back before six passes.

-   Once you win the ball, you have to find a pass. If you cannot pass to an outside player, find a teammate in a position who can.

-   Once the attacking team gets to six passes and have the license to go to goal, the defensive team must stop them playing forward. If they can take the forward pass away, they will have better chance of containing the attacking team and forcing a mistake.

Defensive Exercise 4

There were a number of raised eyebrows when Pep Guardiola described Lionel Messi as "the best defender in the world" in 2013. Rather than thinking of a new position for the Argentine genius, Guardiola simply underlined how important your first line of defense is in the modern game. The most successful coaches in the Champions League over the past five years have added defensive duties to their front players as the emphasis has become to stop the opposition higher up the field. The exercise below has a huge tactical focus and establishes roles, responsibilities, and pressure schemes when defending high up the field.

Set-Up:

The exercise takes place in one half of the field and involves nine players in black shirts, organized with two banks of four along with a goalkeeper, against six players in white shirts, organized with a front two and four midfielders. The two teams' starting positions are below. The team in possession (black shirts) will always start within the width of the 18 yard box. The defending team (white shirts) will always start on the halfway line, with the two forwards in the center circle closest to the goal. The starting positions will also be recovery positions before a restart.

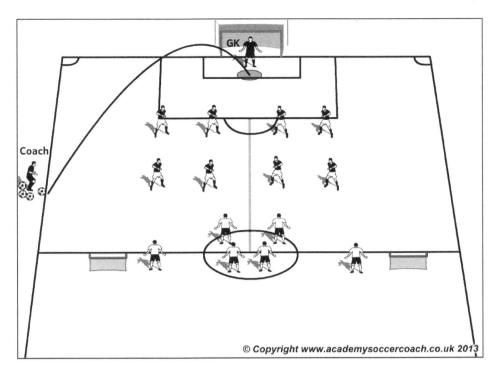

The coach triggers the start of the exercise and serves the ball into the goalkeeper. As soon as the ball is played, the defending team (white shirts) can begin to pressure.

The objective of the team in possession is to work the ball from one side to the other and score in the opposite goal from which the goalkeeper started the play. For example, if the goalkeeper plays to the right back (see below) the goal is to score in Goal 2 on the left side.

The objective for the defending team (white shirts) is to cut off one side of the field with high pressure, and make the play predictable by forcing the team in possession down one side. When they can force a mistake and regain possession, the defending team can then attack the main goal.

Coaching Points:

- High pressure

- "Show" the team in possession down the same side so you must cut off angles of support

- Quick transition into attack to take advantage of winning the ball in an attacking area

- Get into recovery (starting) positions within 20 seconds to keep tempo high.

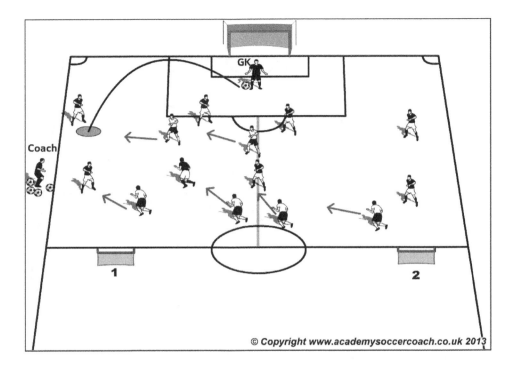

Defensive Exercise 5

Successful teams will always look to create overload situations all over the field, one way or another. Forwards will drop off to add an extra player into the midfield area, midfielders will join in the attack, fullbacks will push on to get beyond wingers. The higher the level you go, the quicker these overloads happen and the more dangerous they will be. This exercise helps defenders prepare for overloads while developing speed, changing direction, getting organized quickly, and blocking shots.

Set-Up:

The exercise takes place on one half of the field and the squad is split into three lines of forwards, two lines of defenders, and a goalkeeper. Speed ladders are used in the lines with forwards and flag poles are used with lines of defenders. If you do not have this equipment, you can use cones.

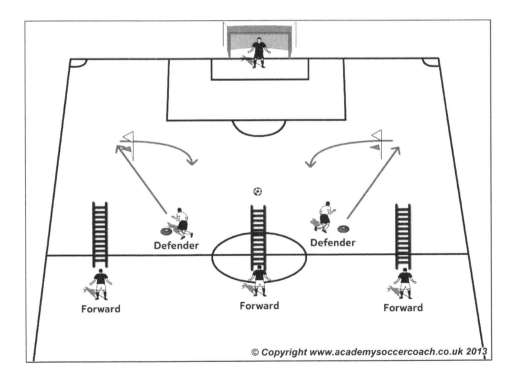

On the coach's signal, all five lines start together. The three forwards must perform dynamic footwork through the speed ladders and there will be a ball waiting for them upon completion. They can then go straight to goal.

The defenders must run around the two flag poles before they can work together and try to stop the three attackers. The attackers have 8 seconds to score so the goal for defenders must be to organize quickly and delay. Once a defender touches the ball, the attack stops and the next group goes. Players recover to the same lines.

Coaching Points:

- Communication! Which forward has the ball and how must defenders organize themselves accordingly?

- "Show" the player on the ball away from goal.

- Take away one of the other two options to try and create a 2v2 situation.

- Do not commit to a tackle or a blocked shot until 100% certain or inside the box.

Summary

It takes a lot to be considered a top class defender today. On top of the physical capabilities like speed and strength, you need the ability to shut down and look after forwards, a great range of passing to start attacks, awareness of danger, as well as concentration and focus to maintain high performance levels game after game, week after week.

Team defending is just as complex. Defenders in the modern game will face so many decision making challenges because the game is more tactical than it ever was. So you must coach defending with a four-dimensional approach because defenders that are vulnerable in any facet of what the game demands will be exposed.

As a modern coach, your ability to 'sell' your players on the importance of team defending will be essential for success. Players today are naturally more inquisitive and will likely question why you want your forwards and midfielders defending with the same vigor as the back four. It is not easy. The modern way requires that all players work harder, work together, take more risks higher up the field, and have a relentless desire to win the ball back. In his column with the Daily Mail on October 5th 2013, Gary Neville praised the blue collar attitude of Bayern Munich when they played Manchester City: "Pep Guardiola has no shame or embarrassment that he wanted his team to be hard working, to sprint to the ball to hunt in packs. 'Squeeze them in!' is the shout we'd hear from the sidelines. The best German and Spanish teams are running all over Premier League teams — not in terms of possession but in terms of organized hard work." You will not be able to do this effectively with your team by using long lectures or by simply yelling and screaming. Players will look at each other and then probably the door.

On the practice field, however, you can turn the skeptics into believers. Your sessions must stress the reward of winning the ball back earlier and how it allows your team to attack against unorganized defenses. Multi-functional exercises that challenge your defenders to think and move quickly will create winning habits that can be taken into a game. If your sessions mirror the challenge and stress of the game itself, your team and defenders will adjust with ease. Always remember that luck is not a strategy and hope is not a method when it comes to keeping shutouts.

8

Transitions

Alarm bells rang in the soccer coaching world when José Mourinho said, "Transitions have become crucial. When the opponent is organized defensively, it is very difficult to score. The moment the opponent loses the ball can be the time to exploit the opportunity of someone being out of position. Similarly when we lose the ball we must react immediately. Everybody says that set plays win most games, but I think it is more about transitions." Could this be the secret to his success? Although the reality is transition is not a new phenomenon in soccer, it has certainly progressed into one of the most important coaching topics in the modern game.

'Transition' refers to the process of changing from attack to defense, or defense to attack. It is a concept that players are usually comfortable defining but are not exposed to enough on the practice field because of the traditional offense versus defense exercises we talked about in Chapter 7. If a phase of an exercise ends as soon as an action is performed like a pass, shot, or 1v1 skill, then transition is absent. Because of this, a number of players and teams, even at the highest level, are exposed in transition.

Transition has also become a hot topic because of how the game has evolved. Since soccer players today are faster and stronger, they can therefore recover more quickly into defending positions than players of a previous era. As the game and players today have gotten faster and more technically efficient, the quicker and more fluidly your team can transition, the better the chance you have of being successful. Spaces in the attacking area of the field are becoming a rare commodity when you play against good teams. You may have the best attacking system in the world, but if your players cannot create space, it will be irrelevant.

Four Dimensions of Transitioning

Developing a team that can transition effectively is no easy task. Players have almost a natural inclination to work harder going forward than they do defensively, as well as wanting to slow the game down when they do regain possession. So how do you change that? The answer (as usual!) is through your work on the practice field. These effective habits have to be ingrained into your players by your exercises, and your coaching. Your work on transitioning must focus on the following four dimensions.

Technical

There is no point in developing endurance, speed, strength, and stamina if a player's technique is flawed. Potential opportunities to transition offensively will be wasted because of inability to possess the ball. Technique is critical to performance in this aspect of the game.

Tactical

Players who are tactically aware and understand their roles, and those of their teammates, really shine in transition. There is no better example in today's game than Sergio Busquets. At the heart of Barcelona's midfield, he does not create headlines for moments of individual brilliance. But when Barcelona pressure and win possession, they typically find Busquets' feet within two passes and he then sets the tempo immediately. He is almost like a conductor who can slow the game down or speed it up with equal ease.

Physical

Your players have to have incredible fitness levels to transition quickly and effectively on both the offensive and defensive sides. Those physical demands must combine endurance with the ability to sprint and change direction in short spaces.

Mental

Effective transition favors the psychological qualities of focus and concentration, but also quick thinkers. David Beckham, a player who was criticized for lacking speed, had a unique ability to spot an attacking player high up the field within seconds of winning possession. Beckham understood where the forwards would make their runs and how they could take advantage of an unorganized defense. He saw pictures on the field a split second quicker than most players and that, along with pinpoint distribution, is what set him apart. Players who receive the ball and then begin to think about their options, usually get caught in possession and then have to do it all over again. A successful transition definitely favors the quick thinkers.

Why Focus On It?

It takes a lot of work for a coach to train a team to be effective in transition. You have to create situations in practice that will help develop your players' game understanding and practice habits. Games have to have an intensity and also challenge players. There are a number of advantages:

- Teams who are effective in transition will attack more against unorganized defenses. When the opposition begins an attack, they typically push players into advanced attacking positions. Upon winning possession and shifting quickly from defense to attack, there is now an opportunity to take advantage of opposition players getting caught out of position. Spaces will open up and this should make it easier to create chances.

- It puts an enormous pressure on the opposition when they are aware that your team excels in transitioning. They will be reluctant to push numbers forward at the risk of getting caught out. This should put less pressure on your defenders with fewer attacking players to worry about.

- The best teams in transition usually set the pace for an up-tempo game. Playing that type of game requires a well-conditioned team. Therefore, your team will be at an immediate advantage if they are conditioned to do this, and should be as much of a threat towards the end of games as they are from the start.

- Because of the physical demands involved in an effective transitioning system, it requires a squad - as opposed to a team. The coach will have to use the bench to maintain this style for 90 minutes plus. This will lead to more involvement and participation from squad players, which will help team spirit as it keeps everyone involved.

Successful Offensive Transitioning

Although transition may seem like a tactical concept because it involves team shape and positioning, it actually requires all four dimensions of modern coaching to be successful. In order for your team to be successful in transition when they gain possession of the ball, the following is required:

- Your team must be well organized defensively before winning possession. If your opponent can draw players out of position before you win possession, you will have fewer opportunities to transition offensively because you will have limited support players.

- Win the ball! The quicker you win the ball back, the better your offensive transition will be. This takes energy and an aggressive mindset, as a team, to force mistakes and win possession.

- The most important pass in transitioning offensively is the first one. If the first pass puts the team back into pressure, you will be surrendering possession straightaway. Make sure the first pass is complete and allows the team to move out of an area of high pressure.

- When transitioning offensively, it is almost natural for players to want to attack the opposition goal as quickly as possible. This sometimes leads to the ball being forced into areas or even individual players losing control when in possession. Good advice for players in this situation is to "Be quick but never rush possession."

- The team that moves off the ball into dangerous areas to offer support will be most successful in transition. This also takes a recognition, by players in possession, of the options they have further up the field. The more they practice these situations, the more comfortable they will become.

Successful Defensive Transitioning

Defensive transitioning is not as glamorous as that for offense but it is just as important. It is sometimes frowned upon in the media as negative because it involves you getting players behind the ball and becoming organized defensively as quickly as possible. This leads to fewer chances for the other team and maybe the game suffers as a spectacle. If you want to be successful, however, you have no choice but to master defensive transitions with your team. In order to do this, the following is required:

- The reaction to giving away possession kills a lot of teams before they even begin defensive transitioning. If a player or a teammate dwells on a mistake, they must try to win the ball back with their team as soon as possible. As a coach, focus on your players' reaction to the mistake rather than the technical error and do not let them 'switch off'!

- You need an aggressive mindset to win possession back as early as possible, but not at the cost of conceding free kicks. Controlled aggression is the key here so that you can make life as hard as possible for the opposition and force mistakes as soon as they gain possession.

- The most important part of defensive transitioning is to stop the opposition playing the ball forward and attacking your team straight away. Try to delay the opposition. If you can force them backwards or sideways, you allow more time to build numbers and help your team defensively.

- If you cannot win the ball back early and you force the opposition back or sideways, your team must get organized as quickly as possible. The best way to measure defensive discipline in your team is to see how quickly you can get numbers behind the ball when you lose possession.

- The higher the level, the less time you will have to transition defensively. Therefore, communication becomes vitally important to get players reorganized and in a position to carry out their defensive responsibilities.

Transition Exercise 1

As soon as the moment of transition occurs, offensively or defensively, your team will have players out of position. As a coach, your aim is to reorganize these players as quick as possible with coaching (players knowing where to go) and with habits (players automatically on the move after transition). This exercise challenges players to deal with inferior numbers, get reorganized quickly, and react successfully to the transition.

Set-Up:

Players are organized into two teams and play 5v5 with goalkeepers on two separate 20x30 yard fields. Players on each 5v5 team, with the exception of the goalkeepers, number themselves 1-4. When the coach calls a number, like "TWO!" in the example below, those players must switch with the players in the same team on the opposite field. Play does not stop during this switch.

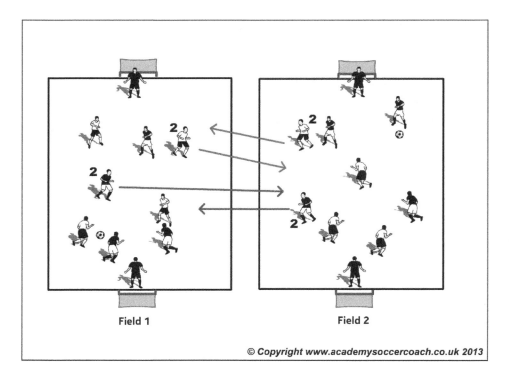

Field 1   Field 2

Coaching Points:

- The quicker the games flow, the greater the challenges for the players so make sure the coach has a good supply of balls for both fields.
- During transition, 'organized chaos' takes over and the team that gets organized quickly will win. Communication from teammates is vital to pass on information to players entering the field.
- Awareness from attacking teams to know they may have an opportunity to go forward with superior numbers if they transition quickly. Alternatively, if they do not have superior numbers, then keeping possession will be key.
- Defensively, if teams can transition quickly, they can use the extra player to pressure aggressively. If they are not successful with a quick transition, the better option would be to delay and simply prevent the team in possession from playing forward.
- Challenge the players who have to transition to understand where their team needs them straight away. This will improve tactical awareness and game management.

Progressions:

- The coach can call two numbers which would then have multiple players in the team transitioning.
- You can make the area bigger which puts a greater physical demand on players.
- A goal can count for three points when scored within five seconds of a transition. This creates a sense of urgency for both teams and individuals to get organized and take advantage of superior numbers.

Transition Exercise 2

This exercise challenges players on their ability to not only keep possession, but to progress possession in a certain direction under pressure. Possession is an important element in transitioning offensively, but only if the ball is moved from an area of high pressure to low pressure. The directionality of the game, along with the constant transitioning, allows the tempo to be high which improves speed of play and fitness levels.

Set-Up:

The exercise takes place in a 20x20 yard square with twelve players divided into two teams of six. Two players from the team in black shirts will be on each side vertically, and two players from the team in white shirts will be on each side horizontally. Two players from each team will start in the middle in a 2v2 scenario. The objective is simple: The two players in the middle are trying to work the ball from one outside line to the other. So, the black shirts are attempting to work the ball up and down the field, while the white shirts are going across the field.

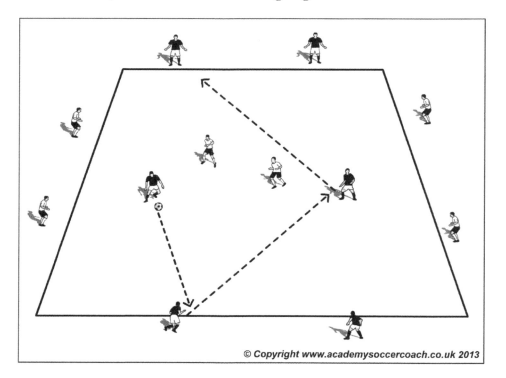

You get one point for every time the ball is transferred from one side to the other without being broken up by the defending players. The players on the outside are limited to two touches and the ball must always be rolling in order to keep the game fast and realistic. Each game lasts three minutes and then the two inside players rotate with two outside players.

There are two potential moments of transition in this game:

1. As soon as the defending team wins possession(offensive).
2. When a point is scored and the team in possession is attempting to score another (defensive).

It is important to recognize those two moments so you can see how players react to these situations - which will determine the success of the exercise.

Coaching Points:

- When the ball is played to the outside players, the two players on the inside must take new positions to look for the next pass.
- Challenge the players on the inside to create space and receive the ball on the half-turn. If they can do this effectively, it will allow them to find an outside player quicker.
- Defensively, this is a full pressure game. If your choice of pressure is medium or low, you will be exposed.
- If a team concedes a point, they must reorganize quickly so that the team in possession does not score successive points. Players who struggle with this will resort to simply watching the ball when instead they should keep pressuring and getting close to the opposition to prevent them from playing forward.

Transition Exercise 3

We have all heard the phrase "You are at your most vulnerable after you have just scored." This is because, too often, after a team scores, players become complacent, switch off mentally, and surrender momentum immediately. This game creates winning habits in transition as it promotes offensive and defensive transitioning within seconds of each other.

Set-Up:

A 30x90 yard field is organized outside the penalty area where the two teams play 5v5 with two goalkeepers. Outside the playing area, there is a wide player on each team who will act as servers, along with a goalkeeper in the middle goal.

The teams play 5v5 with the emphasis on getting numbers into attacking positions and shooting at every good opportunity. Although possession may fluctuate in the game, the first moment of coachable transition will occur when one team scores. This happens below with the team in black shirts.

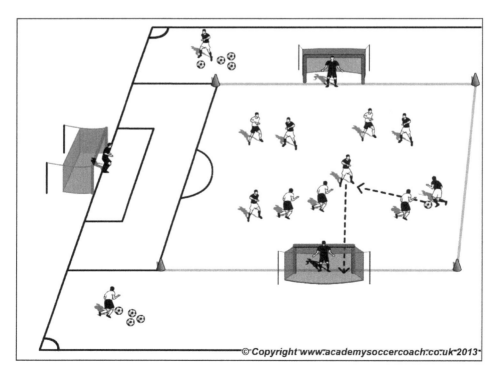

As soon as a goal is scored, the attacking team must send three players into the penalty box where a ball will be served by the wide player within 5 seconds. (The coach should count this time down to encourage players to get into the box quickly.) As soon as the ball is in, three players in the box finish the cross; the team that conceded a goal on the 5v5 game can restart the game from their goalkeeper. This is the defensive transition and will create a 5v2 overload until those three players recover into position.

It is important that you coach within the game and keep it flowing. The coaching points will be:

Mental: Players have to focus and react to moments of transition immediately.

Physical: Players have to get there quickly which means a number of high intensity sprints.

Technical: Players have to execute in key moments of attack and defense.

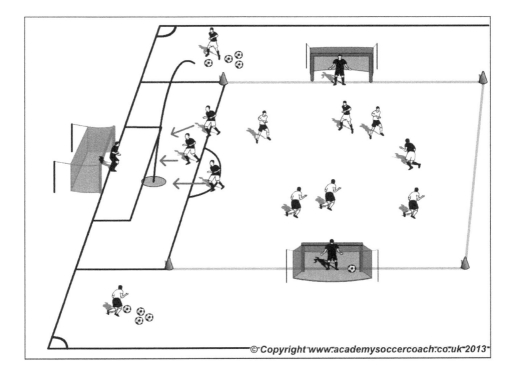

Transition Exercise 4

This exercise challenges players physically to keep up with play and take attacking positions ahead of the ball. The focus here is on the attacking transition as defending teams will usually have time to set and get organized. It is a great exercise for pre-season with a high fitness component, but only if it is performed at a high tempo at all times.

Set-Up:

The field is divided into three zones and there are three teams of five players in each zone, along with two goalkeepers in each goal. The game will start with Team 2 attacking Team 1 and Team 3 will be waiting at the other end. If Team 2 scores, they then go down the other end and attack Team 3. However, if Team 1 wins the ball, they transition out of their zone, towards the other goal, and attack Team 3. Teams are only allowed 5 seconds in the middle zone before attacking so this will keep the tempo high and challenge teammates to keep up with play. Play four three minute sets with one minute recovery in between.

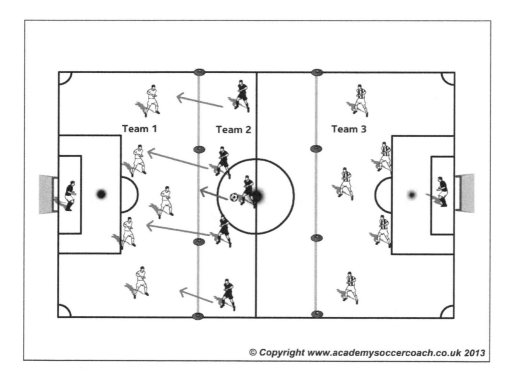

Coaching Points:

-   As soon as the team wins possession and breaks out of defense, it is vitally important that players get into the attacking zone as soon as possible. Do not allow any players to act as holding midfielders and ensure everyone works at optimal speed to support the player with the ball.
-   The player with the ball will typically be the first player to enter the area while supporting teammates arrive. If this player drives into the middle, he/she will be running into trouble. Instead, encourage this attacking player to drive into the attacking area diagonally, so they can move the defenders and create openings for oncoming teammates.
-   The movement of the players with the ball will be key in the attacking area. If all attacking players run in straight lines or even remain static, it will be easier to defend against. Encourage attacking players to take up positions high up the field to stretch the defense and create space for the player on the ball.
-   Be careful this does not turn into a possession exercise in the attacking third. As players become tired, they will look to slow the play down and the defensive team will usually allow it. To prevent this, always encourage penetration by the player on the ball. You can also add a time restriction in the attacking third to keep the tempo high.

Progression

-   Add an all-time target player in each attacking third. Now upon winning possession, the defending team must play the ball over the middle zone and into the target player. This will increase the speed of the game and challenge your players to support the ball quickly.
-   Make the middle zone smaller to allow quicker transitions. The speed of the game should really increase as well as the physical challenges on the players to keep up with play.

Transition Exercise 5

We often think of transitions as mostly occurring in the midfield areas during moments of possession and build-up play. However, games are sometimes won and lost during successful and unsuccessful transitions within twenty yards of goal. This is where the quick thinkers and players with imagination can make a huge difference on the offensive side. This exercise challenges players to think quickly and react to situations where a split second will be the difference between a goal scored or a goal conceded.

Set-Up:

The exercise takes place on a 40x30 yard area. The players are divided into two teams and each team has a goalkeeper. The game is a 2v2 towards goal but the transition aspect is always centered around the restart.

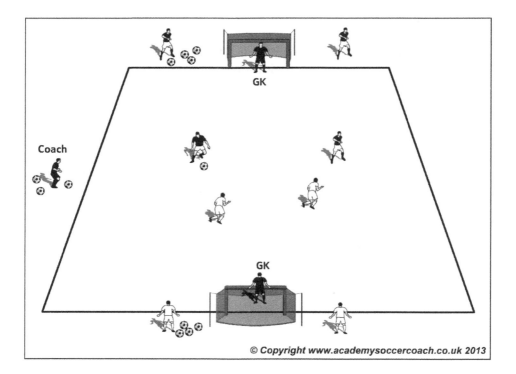

© Copyright www.academysoccercoach.co.uk 2013

Restarts

When a goal is scored, the attacking team stays on and play is restarted right away with a pass from one of the attacking players behind the goal. The two players who just conceded must leave the field and are replaced by two new defensive players right away. This transitional moment challenges the defensive team to get organized and the offensive team to create a goalscoring chance as soon as possible.

If the ball goes out of play from any way other than a goal, the game will restart right away from the coach. Possession is awarded to the opposing team from the one whose player put the ball out of play. Again, failure to transition quickly defensively in this situation will almost certainly lead to an attempt on goal from the attacking team.

Coaching Points:

- With the game being played in and around goal, concentration levels are vital for players involved inside and outside the game. Insist that all players stay engaged throughout the exercise.

- Some players will deal with the transitions better than others, so teammates must help each other out by communicating. This exercise should be loud!

- When the tempo is high, keep quality control on the technical side also. Do not let defenders get into bad habits and at the same time, look for creativity and movement from the attacking players. Keep standards high in all aspects at all times!

Summary

The rewards of mastering transition will take your players to levels they have never been. Quick thinking, alert, and 'always in the right place at the right time' players, are by-products of successfully understanding and implementing effective transition. However, as long as humans play the game, you will never perfect transition. There will be times when you commit too many numbers forward, there will be times when your players give the ball away in dangerous areas, and there will always be simple mental lapses, all of which can prove costly. Although the pursuit of perfection will always be out of reach, the coaches who train using transitional exercises with focus on the right tempo, mental focus, and skill execution, will develop players and teams who excel in this side of the game. Do not let your players be taken by surprise by the speed of a competitive game.

So many coaches talk about the fine margins between winning and losing. Al Pacino passionately told his players, before the big game in the *Any Given Sunday* movie, that they should "claw with their fingernails for that inch." These coaches are not wrong. The higher the level of competition, the more these "inches" are highlighted and often one goal will be the difference between two teams of equal skill levels. If you can help your team create an extra second or two on the ball, while your opponent struggles to recover, you have given them more than an inch. And if that leads to an opportunity to make a difference in the game, you will be rewarded for including transition in your coaching philosophy.

9

Counter Attacking

No matter how good your team is in possession there will be periods of the game during which you will need to defend and get numbers behind the ball. That is the nature of soccer when it is played at the competitive level. You will have spells of possession, they will have spells of possession, and the game will constantly ebb and flow. However, instead of simply absorbing pressure, accepting your fate, and even prolonging those periods of the game, you can still have your team organized in an attacking mindset where they can score in a matter of seconds. This is where counter attacking becomes an art.

The UEFA Technical Report of 2008 described a counter attack as "an attack in reply to an attack" whereas the Canadian Soccer Association went one step further and defined a counter attack as "the gain of possession in the defensive or midfield third where the counter attacking team entered the opponent's defensive third within 15 seconds." It can also be described as a progression from the transition we talked about in Chapter 8.

The value of counter attacking is even more important in the modern game. With detailed analysis available throughout every level of elite soccer, teams are becoming increasingly aware of their opponents' strengths and are now becoming more tactically organized to prevent being exposed in dangerous areas. As a result, defensive organization has become a priority. Even the world's most exciting league has followed suit as the majority of teams in the English Premier League now start the game with only one 'out and out' forward. These systems make it difficult to break teams down and in order to do so, you have to commit numbers forward.

Not Only For Defensive Teams

Counter attacking soccer has often fallen under the label of negative tactics or even anti-football. Johan Cruyff lambasted Chelsea throughout their successful Champions League campaign of 2012. But let's get something clear: there is a big difference in relying on counter attacks and being able to counter attack effectively. Were Manchester United defensive minded when they had Rooney and Ronaldo in attack? Certainly not, but there were a number of teams who felt the full effect of a devastating United counter attack. José Mourinho's teams have always been able to hit teams on the break as the opposition pushed numbers forward into the attack and a staggering 42% of Chelsea's goals from open play in 2006-06 were from the results of counter attacks.

Simply put, as a coach you are not sacrificing your principles and it does not have to be a choice of build-up play against counter attacking styles - unless you choose to make it that way. How many coaches refuse to have counter attacking options in their system because of public perceptions? The same number of coaches are throwing away golden opportunities to attack and create goals.

How we coach counter attacking is critical to the success of our teams. It has now become part of curriculums on coaching courses. The English Football Association, for example, identified six key aspects for coaches to be aware of during their UEFA 'B' License course:

1. **Set Up.** Before even considering using counter attacking as part of your offensive artillery, you need to be organized defensively. The two basic defensive rules of setting up for a counter attack are numbers behind the ball and a collective awareness of where your team will press. Obviously you will need numbers behind the ball to lure in offensive players and catch them off guard when you win possession, but you must decide in what area of the field you will pressure the ball.

2. **Break Up.** This is where you win possession from the opposition to start your counter attack. It can be a tackle, an interception, or even a poor cross that sets your team on its way.

3. **Split Up.** If you gain possession of the ball and look to counter but have all your players tightly congested around the ball, the chances are you will surrender possession right back to the opponents. Make sure your team disperses as soon as you win possession and creates options for the player on the ball.

4. **Play Up.** The player in possession must look to play to forward players as soon as possible during the counter attack. This will make it harder for the opposition to recover and give your team the best chance to attack at speed.

5. **Move Up.** An effective counter attack involves more than one or two players. Players must look to get forward as quickly as possible and try to create an overload in attacking numbers. When you have more numbers forward than defenders, the player in possession has more options.

6. **Security.** There must be a defensive balance to your team, even when on the attack. If you commit too many numbers forward, or leave a part of the field vacant, you are then susceptible to a counter attack directly following your own.

The Four Dimensions of Counter Attacking

It may look easy watching the best teams in the world switch from defending deep in their own half to scoring a goal at the other end in a matter of seconds but as with most things in soccer, it is very complex. You cannot rely solely on skill or athleticism to break teams down at the highest level and the fact that you may only get a limited number of chances per game (via an effective counter attack) means that you need to be aware of these factors in your training. There are so many variables involved in a counter attack, you cannot treat it as an isolated skill.

Technical

The skill components required for effective counter attacking are vital. Arsene Wenger said the most important factor in a counter attack is "the quality of the first pass." You need players who can play under pressure, run with the ball, have the ability to combine with each other, shoot/ finish on goal. Again, these skills may be comfortable to achieve for elite players separately, but are more difficult when time, opponents, and pressure are all added to the equation.

Tactical

Without tactical awareness, your players will fail to see a window of opportunity for a counter attack or worse still, attempt one when they do not have numbers of support - gifting possession in a dangerous area. If your opponents are organized, then the emphasis should be on constructing an attack through possession and build-up play. However, if your opponents are unorganized, the counter attack is on! Players need to be able to know the difference and quickly assess the situation.

Physical

The average counter attacking goal is scored within 10-15 seconds of regaining possession of the ball. If counter attacks start deep in your own half, you can imagine the physical demands needed to attempt more than ten counter attacks per game. Another physical factor worth considering is fatigue. The majority of counter attacks will occur later in the game, when one team starts to commit numbers forward. Your players have to have the capacity to make longer distance, high intensity runs without being affected by fatigue. Again, this means that training intensity over volume will help players become equipped to do this when called upon in games.

Mental

There are a number of cognitive aspects involved in the counter attack. The decision making components will ultimately determine the success of the counter attack, with a unique understanding of individual and tactical features required by players. A player will have to determine when to dribble, when to pass, and where to pass, and typically players in stressful/pressure situations often make poor decisions. Therefore, they need to see these scenarios on the practice field so they can learn how to adapt in a game. There also needs to be a mentality from supporting players to make lung busting runs and accept that they may not get the ball. This is a mentality that you will have to sell to your players during practice. On top of everything, composure is needed to put the finishing touch on the attack and put the ball in the back of the net.

Making Counter Attacking Practices Realistic

Without a connection to game situations, counter attacking exercises can become impractical and therefore players will take minimal information from the session. You cannot coach every kick of the ball during a counter attack simply because every situation can change. The goal during training, therefore, must be to create many counter attacking situations and help players to learn ways to be effective. The following must be included in your session to make counter attacking practices realistic:

Outlet Pass

Once you gain possession of the ball, you should then look for opportunities to change or switch the play and move it away from areas of pressure. This can be done by either dribbling or passing out of pressure, but the ball must go forward. When players are aware that this pass triggers the counter attack, they are more likely to recognize it in a game and adapt their movement accordingly.

Time Constraints

Without using time constraints in your practice session, your counter attacking exercise can quickly become a possession exercise. Challenge the players to be as positive as possible and attack with as much speed as you can. If you are fortunate enough to have pacey players in your team, they will love these exercises. By having a time restriction on your exercises, players will play with a sense of urgency and you are more likely to replicate game-like situations.

Overloads

You want your players to be able to recognize opportunities to counter attack and you also want them to be successful. Therefore, in your practices, you must create as many overload situations as you can so that your players get used to seeing these stimuli in practice, can recognize it in a game, and be confident enough to capitalize on it. The starting points of these overloads will usually happen in areas further down the field, so high intensity runs are an important requirement needed.

Final Product

A counter attack has to finish with a good final product, whether it is a shot on goal or a telling cross. Players must be aware of what they are working towards when they break and this can be a mentality developed on the practice field. Again, a ten pass counter attack with no finish at the end may be easy on the eyes, but is not an effective method of counter attacking. Add a competitive element to your players in their finishing and this should drive quality in front of goal.

Chapter 9

Be Patient With Mistakes!

The variables can change during every counter attack so there will be plenty of mistakes as players deal with when to pass, when to dribble, and what runs to make. The pressure of the situation, along with time, can lead to a lot of mistakes. Be patient with your players during this time as you do not want to take away any creativity from their play. Don't be slow to praise and give your players a reason to make that long distance sprint to get involved in the attack.

Counter Attacking Exercise 1

Although, it can be difficult to replicate a counter attacking exercise in a small-sided game, it is not impossible and this unique exercise challenges players to understand the mentality and mindset of a counter attack in a 3v3 situation. It also challenges both teams to continually attack in an overload situation, where time is a factor, because of the retreating defender. Because of the intensity - fitness and speed become key physical factors.

Set-Up:

Players are organized into two teams of three, playing in a 20x40 yard area with two small goals. There are two 'end zones' located 5 yards from the goal line. Teams play 3v3 with only one restriction: to score, the attacking player has to be inside the 'end zone' and only one defensive player is allowed in, at the same time, to try to prevent the shot on goal. As soon as a shot is attempted, the counter attack can be triggered.

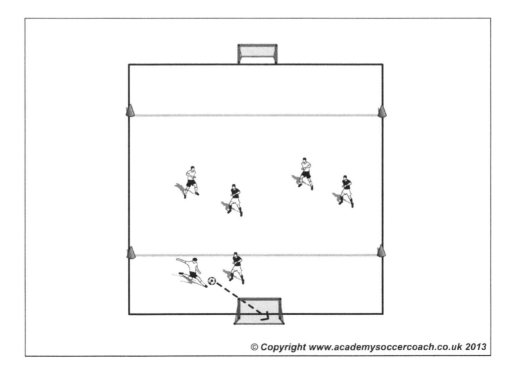

© Copyright www.academysoccercoach.co.uk 2013

As soon as the attacking player attempts a shot on goal, successful or not, they must run around the goal before re-entering the game. The defensive player will take the ball back into play and this will create a 3v2 overload on the other side of the field that should also result in an attack on goal. There is no off-side rule so attacking players should be looking at stretching the field and penetrating off the dribble.

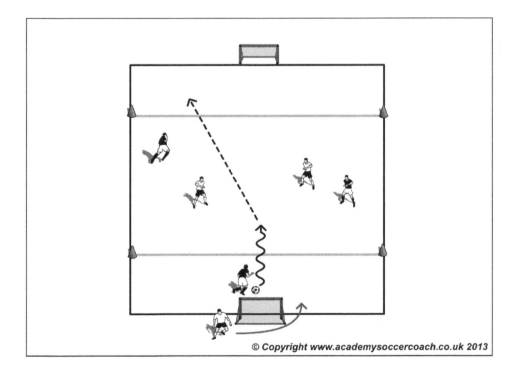

© Copyright www.academysoccercoach.co.uk 2013

Coaching Points:

-   There are a number of ways to score: combination plays, slashing runs, overlaps, or by individual skill. Encourage players to be creative and try as many attacking initiatives as possible.

-   Defensively, this game also creates good habits to never give up. If the defender does not chase the attacking player into the 'end zone', he/she will be at an immediate disadvantage starting the next attack.

-   It is important that you allow players to make their own mistakes going forward but do not let the same mistakes get repeated or allow either team to be predictable going forward.

Counter Attacking Exercise 2

This exercise involves technique, high intensity running, overload in attack versus defense, as well as a game-like situation. Possibly the biggest strength of this exercise, however, is the fact that it combines a structure that allows players to develop habits in sensing when a counter attack is on, alongside the freedom to express themselves once they get in the attacking area. Because of this, you should see different types of finishes and combinations on the way to goal.

Set-Up:

The exercise takes place on three-quarters of a field with two goals, a team divided into defenders and attackers, and two goalkeepers. Attacking players are split into three groups (A, B, and C), while defenders are split into two groups either side of the post (D and E). Play starts from Player A, who chips a pass into the goalkeeper's hands. As soon as the pass is played, Players A and B run around poles 1 and 2, and Players D and E run around poles 3 and 4.

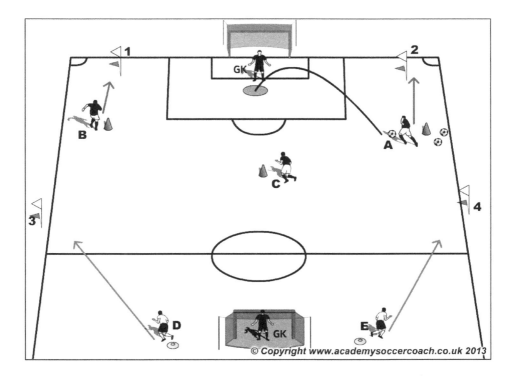

© Copyright www.academysoccercoach.co.uk 2013

When the goalkeeper receives the ball, he/she throws to Player C who turns and attacks the other goal against two recovering defenders, Players D and E. Player C will be joined in the attack by supporting players A and B, creating a 3v2 situation. Offside rules apply.

Coaching Points:

- The movement of supporting players A and B are crucial. If they are slow to get there, Player C will be outnumbered and may lose possession.

- Decision making of Player C. If he/she can penetrate and pull either defender towards the ball, it should open space for supporting players to get ahead of the ball.

- If the defenders decide to hold a high line, supporting players must hold and vary their run. Encourage different runs and communication.

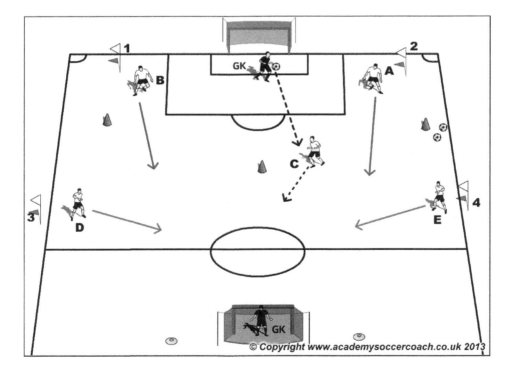

Counter Attacking Exercise 3

This is another exercise that simulates game situations when players counter attack in a 3v2 situation. Technically, it challenges players to start the move with a good outlet pass and physically, the other forwards have supporting runs that must be made at full speed to help create an overload. The mental and tactical components go hand in hand, with decision making, and dealing with whatever movement is initiated by teammates.

Set-Up:

The exercise takes place over just half a field and uses two goals with two goalkeepers. You need four all-time defenders, two defending each goal, and two all-time forwards, with one attacking each goal. The rest of the players are divided into four groups at A, B, C and D.

Play starts at the bottom goal with Player B serving to Forward 1. As soon as the pass is played, Players A and B sprint to support. Defenders 1 and 2 can apply passive pressure to the first pass but as soon as the second pass is made, they can win the ball.

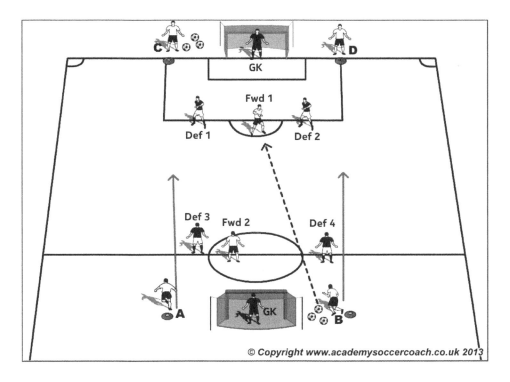

There is now a 3v2 overload towards goal with Players A and B, along with Forward 1, taking on Defenders 1 and 2. As soon as the move finishes, Players A and B exit at the nearest goal, Defenders 1 and 2 and Forward 1 recover. Players C and D now play into Forward 2 and they attack the other goal. The exercise keeps flowing with forwards and defenders rotating after 3 minutes.

Coaching Points:

-   The first pass into the forward must be driven in with pace on the ball. If the ball is floated in, or passed slowly, it will be intercepted in a game.

-   Encourage the two supporting players to make different runs. One should offer the forward an option to drop the pass back, while the other should look to run beyond the forward and stretch the defense.

-   Put a time limit of 8 seconds in place so that there is an urgency in the attack that replicates game tempo.

-   Encourage creativity but stress the importance of a final product – can we create a shot on goal or a penetrating through ball?

-   As the players become more comfortable, allow defenders to win the first ball. This will make the forward have to work hard to hold it until support arrives.

Counter Attacking Exercise 4

You do not have to sit back and wait for a mistake from the opposition for an effective counter attack. Your team can have an aggressive mindset defensively and actively look to counter by pressuring in the right areas. In order to do so, however, your team must be organized and disciplined enough to 'show' your opponents into dangerous areas. This exercise pits a possession team against a counter attacking team and allows your players to see how to take advantage of the opportunities that can arise.

Set-Up:

The exercise takes place from each 18 yard box and involves two teams of seven plus two goalkeepers. There are goals on top of each 18 yard box and two side goals, 3 yards wide using poles (labeled 1 and 2 below).

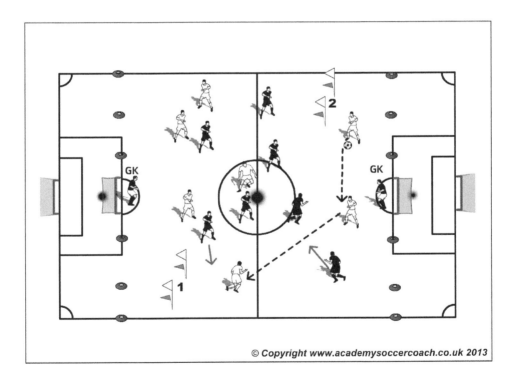

© Copyright www.academysoccercoach.co.uk 2013

The team in white shirts is the possession focused team. They must keep the ball and aim to play in through either side goal 1 or 2, by passing or dribbling. They get a point for each time they do this. They can use either goalkeepers as support to create a 9v7 situation.

Chapter 9

The team in black shirts is the counter attacking team so must pressure the ball and, upon winning it, can attack either goal, and will be rewarded with one point each time they score. The game lasts for three minutes and then the teams switch roles. Physically, this is a difficult game for the counter attacking team but if the tempo drops, the competition element of the exercise will drop also.

Coaching Points:

- The counter attacking team must work together to close down possession. If one player goes, every player should move across and support.

- The transition from attack to defense must be quick. It is likely that the possession team will defend with numbers centrally so the counter attacking team must take advantage of any time and space.

- As soon as the counter attacking team wins possession, challenge the player on the ball to find a player in space as quickly as possible.

- If the counter attacking team wins the ball in a congested area, look to switch play and attack the other goal. To do this, there must be an awareness and players willing to move into space.

- Pressure the goalkeeper! This is a key outlet for the possession team and if they can even affect the service, they may win the ball.

- You can add an extra challenge to the possession team where each switch of play must involve either goalkeeper.

Counter Attacking Exercise 5

To transfer counter attacking from the practice field to a game, players need to recognize cues and opportunities to break as quickly as possible. This exercise changes the picture slightly as it starts the counter attack from a wider area than most practice exercises do. It challenges players to think more about effective movement so they can still provide that final product before a defense gets organized.

Set-Up:

Two 20x10 yard grids are set up either side of the halfway line. Teams are divided into two teams of five players and one goalkeeper. Four players in each team start the exercise in one grid and one player from each team (target player) starts centrally, 20 yards from goal. The white team starts with the ball and after three passes, they can play to their target player (A) and then go to goal. The target player in the other team becomes a defender. Two players from the white team can go and support their teammate and one player from the black team can go and help defend, creating a 3v2 towards goal. When the attack finishes, the next ball will start with the black team on Grid 2.

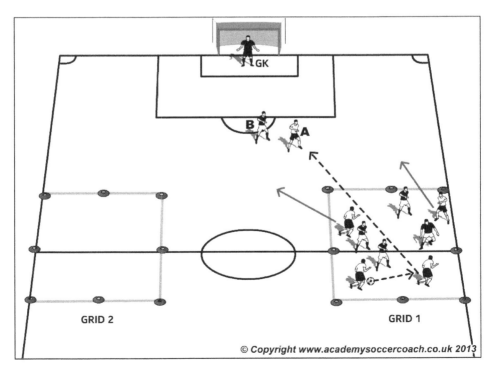

Coaching Points:

- The possession element has to be with the outlet ball in mind, so awareness and the body shape of players in possession is crucial. Look for players to create a yard of space and open their body up to hit the target player.

- The type of pass into the outlet player needs accuracy and weight. It needs to be played to the left shoulder of the target forward so the supporting runners can get either side of him/her. Also, if there is no pace on the ball, it will force the target player to check in closer to the grid and the supporting runners will struggle to stay onside.

- The supporting runs must be made as soon as the entry pass is played to the target forward in order to break quickly.

- If the target forward has the ability to play the supporting players effectively on one touch, it will make it harder for the recovering defenders to stop the attack.

Progressions:

- Increase the pass requirement to 4 or 5 to challenge the players' ability in possession.

- Move the grids further back to make the supporting runs longer, challenging the players physically.

- Add a player from each side in the alternate grid and then give the attacking team the option of using the weak side.

- Add a defender so that the target player is now outnumbered and must hold the ball for the supporting players to join in the attack.

- Add a time limit for the team in possession to score.

- If the defensive team wins the ball in the grid, they can play out to the target player, now adding a transition element to the exercise.

Summary

In order to be an effective counter attacking team, you as the coach, must embrace it in your philosophy and your work. Remember there is 'attacking' in the title for a reason so you must think positively about the potential benefits for your team. Similar to being successful in transition, the ability to turn defense into attack is worth its weight in gold when you play against teams who specialize in getting organized efficiently.

Counter attacking is about concentration in recognizing when to break, teamwork in moving forward, speed in exploiting space left by defense, and the ruthlessness to finish off the move. When everything goes right, it can be poetry in motion. But like everything else, it is a process. There will be times when you overcommit, times when the player in possession chooses the wrong option, and times when one of your players will miss a wide open chance. How you manage these mistakes will be key to your team's success. If players feel that the opportunity for criticism outweighs the opportunity for success, you will see less and less players sprinting long distances to get involved in the attack and maybe even fewer forward passes upon retaining possession in the first place. Balance is the key with coaching counter attacking, in so many areas, but none are more important than how you deal with errors. It is not easy but remember this... when your team is defending deep in your half one moment and 12 seconds later, the ball is the back of your opponent's net, it will have all been worth it!

10

Measuring our Work

So there you have it. We have put our training program together, and your players are ready for the technical, physical, tactical, and mental demands of the game. So the result should take care of itself, right? Not so fast.

Your job as the coach now needs to focus on how to put everything together and make sure that the players 'buy in' to your philosophy; they need to be ready to fully commit themselves to not only your sessions, but your vision. If you want to extract as much from your players individually, and collectively, there has to be a focus on the bigger picture. If the effort ends when the players jump in the car, when they do not have a lifestyle conducive to that of a top level athlete, the sessions will have been wasted.

You must extend your work to inspire and impact your player's lifestyle habits. That is where the top coaches today separate themselves. How do players at Manchester United and AC Milan manage to prolong their careers? By creating an environment that encourages players to commit their lives to looking after their bodies and becoming better athletes. And the coach/manager establishes, controls, and drives this environment by having an influence on their players long after they leave practice. Rules and enforcement will only drive the short term. Even though the cones are picked up and the players have left the field, you still have the colossal task of influencing their behavior.

If it sounds like a big job, that's because it is. High level coaching becomes a lifestyle – focused on you and your players. That is the only way to be successful in the modern game. In the past, a coach was a boss who relied on positional power to lead. Today's coaches must be partners with their players. You simply cannot do it on your own and there are no half measures when you are committing yourself. Sir Alex Ferguson said it best: "Don't do it part time. You have to live your life and that of the players." Part of being successful is accountability - so when you take charge remember this. It is time to take responsibility as to why everything involved with your team is not first class and improve as many aspects as possible. To make this change possible, take as many players with you as you can. They'll come if they see meaning in it for them to become involved. So make it meaningful for them!

The 10 Common Traits of a Modern Coach

Teams are complex; intricate groups of different individuals who naturally develop their own rules and habits. The best coaches make sure these habits are good ones and are sustained. Vision and strong leadership are required to cultivate winning behaviors. Modern coaches, today, may all be successful but they are not defined by wins and medals. They may be working at different levels and have different tactical approaches, but when you study them closely, they all share these ten common traits.

1. Lifelong Learners

Coaches today must not only be a student of the game, but also keep up with the latest trends in sport, psychology, business, and technology. A thirst for knowledge and a desire to learn from the best are critical for success because the top coaches are always looking to improve and examine better ways to give feedback to players. Some of the top coaches today share similar backgrounds in education outside the game. José Mourinho and Ottmar Hitzfeld were both PE teachers before starting off as coaches, whereas Louis van Gaal was a qualified gymnastics instructor.

We live in a world where important information and research is just a click away but finding it and using it are two different things entirely. You must also identify and prioritize future developments so you can keep adding to your understanding of how to improve performance. Once identified, these new ideas have to be consistently applied to your coaching; this becomes key.

Remember, knowledge is not power until it is used so you must have the willingness to act upon what you have learned. Sometimes the most difficult task, however, is not getting new innovative concepts into your coaching, but instead getting the old ones out. A four dimensional exercise will not have an effect on your training program if you follow it with a long distance run or a long winded lecture.

Modern coaches commit to learning, applying, reviewing, and improving on a day to day basis. During the reviewing process, you should second guess everything. Do you have a set of favorite practices that you regurgitate with every group you work with? Do players know what you will be doing every day at practice? These are questions worth considering. If practices are always the same it becomes easier and the players benefit less. Effective training requires unusual stress through frequent change. Alternating sessions and exercises can reduce boredom in practice (which drains the energy levels of players). You do not need 1,000 different exercises to become a top coach, but you do need to have the ability to change and update sessions to meet all the demands of the players. What worked for one group of players may not work for another. These demands will improve your team but also progress how you think as a coach. If you are not making significant efforts to continually improve as a coach, the chances are that you are falling behind rather than staying the same.

2. Lead by Example

If you want to influence and lead your players, which the top modern coaches do every day, you must practice what you preach. You have to employ a high quality control in life as well as the game. The days of "do as I say, not as I do" are gone. I firmly believe that a modern coach should commit himself/herself to a healthy lifestyle because it has two positive effects. Firstly, the players will relate more to a coach who looks as though they hold the same standards as they do. Secondly, it takes enormous amounts of energy and vigor to be a modern coach. If you are dragging during a game, meeting, or session, your impact will be reduced and you will not achieve your goals.

No matter how good your session plans are, without enthusiasm, energy, and focus, it will not have maximum effect. Stay fresh in mind and body and keep growing as a coach so you can be an example to your players. Show them that good enough is never good enough, in every aspect of the game. You will be amazed how that rubs off on their approach to the game. Always remember, 'You are your own message'. If you want your players to be punctual, be the first one there every day. If you want your players to do extra practice, stay behind with them once a week. It is the little examples from the coach that drive the culture of a program.

3. Obsessed!

Training to become a master at coaching requires the same practice and diligence it takes to become a professional athlete or musician. Without an obsessive desire to reach the top, you are not likely to put in the hours required or be able to deal with the setbacks that will invariably occur. Time is so important in today's sports climate and coaches plead for it when they get a new position. They need time to build relationships, to organize their team, to work on the practice field, to sign new players, and to deal with commercial work that goes along with the game. It can get to a stage where there are not enough hours in the day. In 2013, 72% of participants in the Annual Castrol LMA European Managers and Coaches Survey described their "participation in the game to be obsessive". The definition of obsessive may be relative to the coach but many times it includes sleepless nights, stress, and thinking about solutions to problems when you should be relaxing!

Preparation is a huge element also, and because modern coaches have to keep evolving to stay ahead of the game, you will never master it. You can, of course, be obsessed with the wrong things, like winning and power, but if you are fixated with developing as a coach and improving the performance of your players, it is perfectly healthy. Success in sport has always been driven by perspiration rather than inspiration. The best coaches and players live by this mantra of hard work, day after day, and week after week.

4. Focus on the Process

When you deal with elite players, results matter. That is how your work will be judged by the outside world. However, even though modern coaches are successful, the wins and trophies are a byproduct of their work rather than the sole focus. They are not consumed by the outcome, but instead driven by what produces the results.

A coach who is focused on the process believes that the game is won on the practice field, rather than the game field. Therefore, a modern coach will spend more time planning his/her training session than they will delivering it. You must live by the saying, "If you focus on results you will never change. If you focus on change you will get results."

Modern coaches are also more empathic towards the players and do not let their results define them as people. This approach typically creates a respect and loyalty from the players and is a reason why coaches like Pep Guardiola are loved by the squad, despite having to leave key players on the bench every week. Nurture your players and they will produce consistent performances. Alternatively, if you treat your players in accordance to the results you achieve, you will see their performances fluctuate at the same rate of your mood swings. This is a no-brainer but requires emotional intelligence from you, the coach, to say and do the right thing and not necessarily react to how you are feeling. There is a difference.

Although we live in a demanding society, there is no quick way to the top. You can push yourself and have enormous ambition in the game but patience is needed alongside it as everything takes time. It may look as though Jose Mourinho became an instant success at Chelsea, but he honed his coaching skills under Sir Bobby Robson at Porto and Barcelona. Failure can be a valuable part of this process too as most successful coaches have been fired/sacked in an early part of their career. This failure has inspired them to come back even better. To make it in the top level of soccer coaching, your levels of persistence have to be greater than your levels of ambition.

5. Establish a Clear Philosophy

Modern coaches work from the end backwards. If you are going to take your players on a journey, make sure you know *where* you are going, along with how to deal with the challenges that you will face. The best coaches have a clearly defined philosophy that can inspire and motivate teams in the long run. This philosophy outlines not only how they play, but also how they will work with the players, approach discipline, and what areas will be targeted as focal points to their success.

This philosophy is not a simple "pass and move" or "we want to play like Barcelona" but rather a business type strategy that determines how the program will run. Andre Villa Boas told LMA Manager Magazine in September 2013, "You have to set out clear objectives and common rules and show that you have belief in your players. If you have any doubt when you step out onto that training ground, the players will sense it."

When issues arise, on or off the field (and they always do!), your framework of success will guide how you approach them. The importance of this is that you always refer to the system and do not rely on the emotion of the moment. Brendan Rodgers has made a name for himself as a coach with progressive ideas on how the game is played. Below you can see his framework for decision making and the principles of the game which he keeps on display at Melwood, Liverpool's practice facility. Rodgers' philosophy is there for all his players to see, and because of this they are in no doubt as to what is expected in every facet of the game.

Decision Making and the Principles of the Game

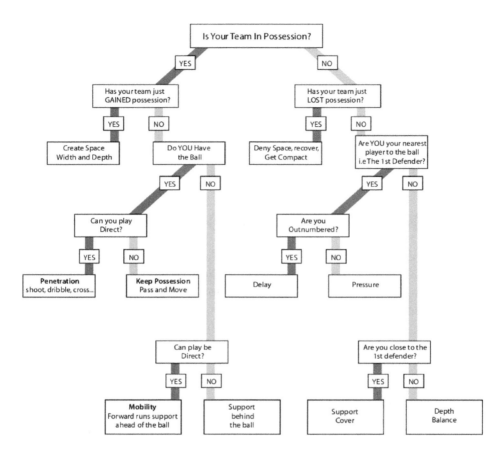

If you want to really build your philosophy and decide how you will work, get used to writing things down. It may take up time and your players may not even see it, but it will be reflected in your work. Goalsgonesocial.com believes that people in the business world, who write their goals down earn nine times more income. It means you have a purpose, you are organized, and you are prepared for what is ahead. You are turning dreams into plans – something tangible that you can now work towards. Everything should be recorded from your sessions, to your philosophies, to your goals.

Below is Rui Faria's (José Mourinho's longtime assistant coach) training model that he shared at the NSCAA Course in August 2012. 'Specific

Exercises' refers to his selection of training exercises, which should always be consistent with the way you would like to play. 'Competitive/ Intensity' creates concentration and awareness for the players. The 'Details of the Sessions' includes space, number of players, and principles. 'Pattern and Repetition' referred to the organization of what tactical element they were looking to work on that week. The end result was 'Creation of Habits' which they believed would take them through games with the desired level of performance and result.

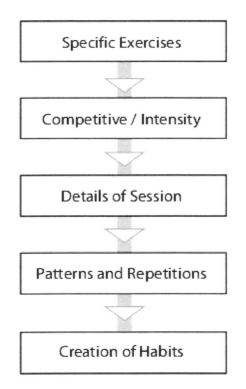

6. The Art of Communication

Without a shadow of a doubt, the most important aspect of coaching is communication. You may work with soccer players, but you coach people and the importance of your relationships with them is paramount. Once you have the knowledge, you must be able to transfer your ideas and intent towards your players.

The information that you pass on to your players has to be clear and concise. A passionate message that lacks clarity will fall on deaf ears. We often hear of head coaches and managers who have 'lost the dressing room'. This usually means that the players are no longer on-board with their ideas and tune out every message that they try to transmit to them. This is simply a result of a lack of communication, which leads to anger and disunity throughout the team so you must build bridges with your players and not walls.

On the training field, language is a huge challenge in the modern game. The players must understand what the coach is saying so it is vital not to bombard them with coaching jargon or simply talk in soccer clichés. Feedback must be specific before it can be acted upon and an abundance of information usually means scarcity of attention. Timing is also a huge factor in successful communication for a modern coach. During the heat of the game, with emotions high, coaching points must be clear and concise for the player to take them on-board.

How you treat players is an integral part of communication as well as a reflection of your values. Quite simply, they deserve your time and respect. Honesty, more than anything else, will make or break your credibility as a coach. There will be times when you have to tell a player something that they may not like but certainly need to hear. This can strengthen your relationships with players as difficult conversations provide an opportunity to build credibility and trust. Have the courage to be clean and honest, but not to the point of being brutal or destructive to confidence. Former England sports psychologist, Bill Beswick, believes that often unknowingly, a coach will talk to his star players seven times more than the others. A key to fostering team spirit is appreciating all your players, not just the stars.

Another variable that can change when discussing communication in the modern game is the profile of players. If you think working with the best players in the world is easy, you are very much mistaken. These players are conditioned to survive in a very competitive environment. Egos must be kept in check and conflicts must be resolved. Every day, their self-belief is challenged. In order to do this successfully, you must handle conflict quietly. With so many media outlets available, it does not take long for arguments to be turned into 'training ground bust-ups' and then transfer requests. A modern coach will never criticize his players in public and will always deal with discipline quickly and quietly.

Awareness of the power of social media can be a huge strength for a modern coach. Coaches like Carlo Ancelotti and Michael Laudrup can use the post-game or pre-game interviews to make a statement to their fans, owners, players and even the global audience. Thousands of coaches may not have the same type of media channels available, but they do have one valuable way of connecting with people who have a direct interest in your work. Some coaches view Twitter or Facebook as a threat, but I think they have the capability to allow your coaching to be as visible as possible. We can complain about young players today communicating in a different way than our generations did, but this will not have any effect on our influence over them. Instead, we should embrace every avenue in which we can communicate and make it as positive as possible. No complaining about circumstances or bemoaning luck – once you take the attitude that you create your own destiny through hard work and smart work, your players will follow suit. You do not have to be aggressive with it but at the same time, give them as many reminders as possible.

Always remember, communication is not just words. Everything communicates, even when you don't speak. Great coaches understand the power of silence. Respect your players enough to listen to them and learn what is important to them. Howard Wilkinson summed it up perfectly when he said: "If you are not positively affecting the behavior of your players, you are not a coach. And if you don't change the way they think and feel, you won't change the way they behave."

7. A Great Support System

The pursuit of excellence in the game of soccer is far from easy. The obsession can play havoc with your personal life and it can be almost one huge balancing act involving hard work and recovery.

The pressures of the game and time demands can have damaging effects on your health and your relationships so you have to be careful to have some balance in your life. Just like your players, you cannot get the best out of yourself alone.

We often stress the importance of family and friends to our players in their lives, but the same applies to a coach. Your support system will play a large role in your ability to manage the lifestyle of a top coach. Firstly, a great support system will always give you perspective. It is only a game and after we discuss how our team is struggling with a certain aspect of the game, it does not take long to look at that problem in relation to others in the world. Secondly, a great support system will have enormous levels of patience. Spouses/partners of coaches have to put up with a lot: dinners will regularly be delayed, cancelled, or you may be there in body only as he/she sees you staring off in space before the appetizer arrives. Although family and friends will go 'above and beyond' for you, make sure you do not take them for granted. Make time for family events, spend time with friends, and always have a balanced outlook in life. All coaches need the support, encouragement, and mentoring of others. The best coaches have gurus in the game to whom they can pick up the phone and ask for advice.

8. Deal with Setbacks

Unless you have incredible luck or are only in the game for a short time, you will experience significantly more lows than highs. Soccer is famous for its dramatic failures and you will be no different.

How you deal with these highs and lows are of upmost importance to your team. You do not get bonus points for being upset and you are not a better coach because you take defeat worse than anyone else. In fact, if you cannot get over defeat quickly enough you may experience it again very soon because of the impact your behavior will have on your team.

Manchester United once had a team goal throughout the season that they would never lose two games in a row. This approach meant that as soon as they lost a game (which was not very often) they immediately looked forward to winning the next one. This also allows players to 'stay in the moment' and focus on what they can control. Similarly, winning can test the temperament of a coach as complacency usually sneaks in the back door when teams start looking at finals, rankings, or anything beyond the next game.

Reality will tell you that you cannot win every game but you can always win the next one. Top coaches today have the ability to bounce back after a set-back and rise to the next occasion. Recovering, refocusing, and getting back to business is a learnable skill. It is a weakness to get caught up in either praise or criticism so the best approach is to keep a ceiling on the victories, a floor on the defeats, and the appropriate short distance between the two.

9. Don't Take the Easy Route

We know that the traditional approach to soccer coaching does not give us the outcomes that we desire. It has been proven both in standards and results. This approach simply coaches players in the exact same way we were coached ourselves – different generations but same styles. It is the presumption that once you collect knowledge, our players should do exactly what we want them to do and in the manner that we want them to do it. But this could not be further from the truth.

Gone are the days when yelling and screaming at players is an effective way to get them to perform. Doing what was done yesterday, or doing it only 5% better is no longer a formula for success because of the rate at which modern coaches are developing. There has to be a huge amount of courage for coaches today with so much pressure and difficult decisions to make. You must always do the right thing as opposed to the easy thing if you want to gain credibility amongst your staff and players.

What will separate you from traditional coaches are not your new ideas, but rather your implementation of them. Nothing can take the place of experience on the field with players. Seeing what works, or more importantly what does not work, takes the experience of working with players every day. Simply put, do as much as you can, as often as you can and you will progress quickly. In every practice session, be as concerned about your standards, as well as those of your players. You can tell everyone you had "another great session" with your players, knowing that you did the same exercises that you always did. Why would it not be great?! The players are not likely to tell you otherwise. Instead raise the bar and take every session to a new level.

10. And Remember to Enjoy It!

At the end of the day, this is what coaching is: a journey of transforming potential into performance. It is amazing what can get done with energy, activity, and a willingness to accomplish. When you add enthusiasm to your coaching, the response and acceptance from players is phenomenal. It is important that your players like you because there is a better chance they will respect you and listen to what you have to say. If you have a fun side to your personality let it shine through in your coaching. Don't try to be like everyone else. Be yourself. Enthusiasm is like a magnet, pulling players towards you. Practice should be a fun place to be, where players can grow, learn, compete, work hard, and obtain a sense of achievement.

Dare to be different. Coaching is not about creating clones so look to distinguish yourself at all times. Unless there is something unique about the way you coach, you will end up competing with other coaches on win/loss records alone and that is not how modern coaches attract people's attention. Great coaches evolve over time based on their dedication to the game and willingness to adapt at the same rate at which the game does. Arrigo Sacchi once said, "As long as humanity exists something new will come along – otherwise football dies." In today's soccer world, that time has arrived and a coaching revolution is quietly taking place. The coaches most responsive to change will be the most successful in the next ten years.

After reading this book, you now have to decide what direction you want to go. Each coach's journey is different. You can focus on results, make practice miserable, do not connect with your team, rule by fear, and use the same sessions you have always used. Or you can be an optimist, have a go, and dream as big as you did when you began playing the game. Good luck, enjoy the ride, and make the experience as much fun for your players as it is for you!

The Modern Soccer Coach: Position-Specific Training by Gary Curneen

Aimed at football coaches of all levels, and players of all ages and abilities, The Modern Soccer Coach: Position-Specific Training seeks to identify, develop, and enhance the skills and functions of the modern soccer player whatever their position and role on the pitch.

This book offers unique insight into how to develop an elite program that can both improve players and win games. Filled with practical no-nonsense explanations, focused player drills, and more than 40 illustrated soccer templates, this book will help you – the modern coach - to create a coaching environment that will take your players to the next level.

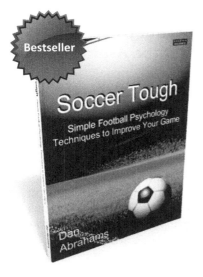

Soccer Tough: Simple Football Psychology Techniques to Improve Your Game by Dan Abrahams

"Take a minute to slip into the mind of one of the world's greatest soccer players and imagine a stadium around you. Picture a performance under the lights and mentally play the perfect game."

Technique, speed and tactical execution are crucial components of winning soccer, but it is mental toughness that marks out the very best players – the ability to play when pressure is highest, the opposition is strongest, and fear is greatest. Top players and coaches understand the importance of sport psychology in soccer but how do you actually train your mind to become the best player you can be? Soccer Tough demystifies this crucial side of the game and offers practical techniques that will enable soccer players of all abilities to actively develop focus, energy, and confidence. Soccer Tough will help banish the fear, mistakes, and mental limits that holds players back.

Scientific Approaches to Goalkeeping in Football: A practical perspective on the most unique position in sport
by Andy Elleray

Do you coach goalkeepers and want to help them realise their fullest potential? Are you a goalkeeper looking to reach the top of your game? Then search no further and dive into this dedicated goalkeeping resource. Written by goalkeeping guru Andy Elleray this book offers a fresh and innovative approach to goalkeeping in football. With a particular emphasis on the development of young goalkeepers, it sheds light on training, player development, match performances, and player analysis. Utilising his own experiences Andy shows the reader various approaches, systems and exercises that will enable goalkeepers to train effectively and appropriately to bring out the very best in them.

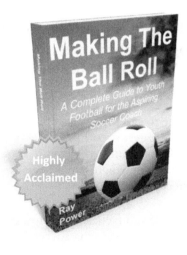

Making The Ball Roll: A Complete Guide to Youth Football for the Aspiring Soccer Coach by Ray Power

Making the Ball Roll is the highly acclaimed, complete guide to coaching youth soccer.

This focused and easy-to-understand book details training practices and tactics, and goes on to show you how to help young players achieve peak performance through tactical preparation, communication, psychology, and age-specific considerations. Each chapter covers, in detail, a separate aspect of coaching to give you, the football coach, a broad understanding of youth soccer development. Each topic is brought to life by the stories of real coaches working with real players. Never before has such a comprehensive guide to coaching soccer been found in the one place. If you are a new coach, or just trying to improve your work with players - and looking to invest in your future - this is a must-read book!

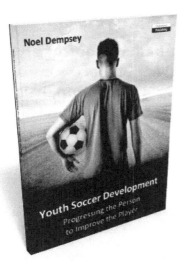

Youth Soccer Development: Progressing the Person to Improve the Player by Noel Dempsey

In "Youth Soccer Development", football coach Noel Dempsey examines where coaching has come from and where it is heading. Offering insights into how English football has developed, coaching methods, 'talent' in youngsters, and how a player's entire environment needs to be considered in coaching programmes - this book offers many touchpoints for coaches who want to advance their thinking and their coaching. Leaving specific onfield drills and exercises to other books, "Youth Soccer Development" digs deep into 'nature versus nature', players' core beliefs, confidence, motivation, and much more. Advocating that to improve the player, you must improve the person, Dempsey puts forward a case for coaches to be realistic with their players, ensure that they work positively across all facets of their lives - especially education - and to instil a mindset that leads to players being the best person they can be.

Developing the Modern Footballer through Futsal by Michael Skubala and Seth Burkett

Aimed at coaches of all levels and ages, Developing the Modern Footballer through Futsal is a concise and practical book that provides an easy-to-understand and comprehensive guide to the ways in which futsal can be used as a development tool for football. From defending and attacking to transitional play and goalkeeping, this book provides something for everyone and aims to get you up-and-running fast.

Over 50 detailed sessions are provided, with each one related to specific football scenarios and detailing how performance in these scenarios can be improved through futsal. From gegenpressing to innovative creative play under pressure, this book outlines how futsal can be used to develop a wide range of football-specific skills, giving your players the edge.

The Footballer's Journey: real-world advice on becoming and remaining a professional footballer by Dean Caslake and Guy Branston

Many youngsters dream of becoming a professional footballer. But football is a highly competitive world where only a handful will succeed. Many aspiring soccer players don't know exactly what to expect, or what is required, to make the transition from the amateur world to the 'bright lights' in front of thousands of fans. The Footballer's Journey maps out the footballer's path with candid insight and no-nonsense advice. It examines the reality of becoming a footballer including the odds of 'making it', how academies really work, the importance of attitude and mindset, and even the value of having a backup plan if things don't quite work out.

Deliberate Soccer Practice: 50 Passing & Possession Football Exercises to Improve Decision-Making by Ray Power

Aimed at football coaches of all levels, but with a particular emphasis on coaches who work with youth players, *50 Passing & Possession Football Exercises to Improve Decision-Making* is comprised of 20 Technical Practices and 30 Possession Practices. They are carefully designed to be adaptable to suit the needs of the players you work with; to challenge them and give them decisions to make. The sessions look to make soccer complex and realistically difficult – no passing in queues from one cone to the next with no interference. Crucially, the exercises offer a means to accelerate player development effectively and enjoyably. Part of the *Deliberate Soccer Practice* series.

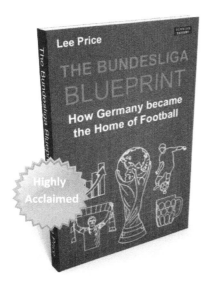

The Bundesliga Blueprint: How Germany became the Home of Football by Lee Price

In this entertaining, fascinating, and superbly-researched book, sportswriter Lee Price explores German football's 10-year plan. A plan that forced clubs to invest in youth, limit the number of foreign players in teams, build success without debt, and much more. The Bundesliga Blueprint details how German fans part-own and shape their clubs, how football is affordable, and the value of beer and a good sausage on match days. The book includes interviews from Michael Ballack, Jens Nowotny and Christoph Kramer, and the movers-and-shakers behind Germany's leading clubs including Schalke, Dortmund, and Paderborn.

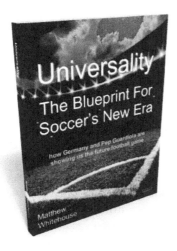

Universality | The Blueprint for Soccer's New Era: How Germany and Pep Guardiola are showing us the Future Football Game by Matthew Whitehouse

The game of soccer is constantly in flux; new ideas, philosophies and tactics mould the present and shape the future. In this book, Matthew Whitehouse – acclaimed author of The Way Forward: Solutions to England's Football Failings - looks in-depth at the past decade of the game, taking the reader on a journey into football's evolution. Examining the key changes that have occurred since the turn of the century, right up to the present, the book looks at the evolution of tactics, coaching, and position-specific play. They have led us to this moment: to the rise of universality. Universality | The Blueprint For Soccer's New Era is a voyage into football, as well as a lesson for coaches, players and fans who seek to know and anticipate where the game of the future is heading.

Soccer Tough 2: Advanced Psychology Techniques for Footballers by Dan Abrahams

In Soccer Tough 2: Advanced Psychology Techniques for Footballers Dan introduces soccer players to more cutting edge tools and techniques to help them develop the game of their dreams. Soccer Tough 2 is split into four sections – Practice, Prepare, Perform, and Progress and Dan's goal is simple – to help players train better, prepare more thoroughly, perform with greater consistency and progress faster.

Each section offers readers an assortment of development strategies and game philosophies that bring the psychology of soccer to life. They are techniques that have been proven on pitches and with players right across the world.

The Volunteer Soccer Coach: 75 Training Games for Outstanding Attacking Play by James Jordan

Are you a volunteer soccer coach with a full time job outside football? Then this book is for you! Utilising a game-based approach to soccer – where individuals actually play games rather than growing old in semi-static drills – author James Jordan offers 75 cutting-edge exercises across 15 detailed session plans which help players develop an attacking mindset, improve their skills, and, most of all, nurture a love for soccer. Through his approach, James has won six High School State Championships and one Classic 1 Boys' Club Championship over the past decade. Aimed at coaches of both young male and female players, from 5-18 years of age, and adaptable depending on age group and skill set, each illustrated session plan is organized in an easy-to-understand format.

A Special Book

Soccer Roy: First Touch
by Erin Curneen, Gary Curneen, Garth Bruner

Please let me introduce you,
To a joyful baby boy,
With big blue eyes and a welcoming smile,
He goes by the name of Roy.

Gary and Erin Curneen wrote this children's book to forever honor their son Roy, who lived a brief life, and to give back to the hospital that gave them three weeks with their baby boy. Erin gave birth to Roy on December 3, 2014, and he was immediately taken into the care of Children's Hospital Los Angeles, due to a congenital diaphragmatic hernia. Even though Roy could not be saved, Gary and Erin were overwhelmed by the care that their son received and felt a strong urge to give back in some way. Their hope is that Roy's memory can forever make a difference in the lives of children. **All profits received from this book will be donated to Children's Hospital Los Angeles.**

Thank you very much for purchasing this copy of *The Modern Soccer Coach*.

At Bennion Kearny, it is our intention to try to provide the best soccer coaching and football-related books that we possibly can, and for that matter we are always happy to receive readers' feedback.

So, please feel free to email me – James – and let me know your thoughts!

James   James@BennionKearny.com

Learn More about our Books at:

www.BennionKearny.com/Soccer